LADY MARY WROTH: POEMS

RENAISSANCE TEXTS AND STUDIES

LADY MARY WROTH
POEMS

A MODERNIZED EDITION

Edited by R. E. Pritchard

KEELEUNIVERSITY**PRESS**

First published in 1996
by Keele University Press
Keele University, Staffordshire, England

© The contributor and KUP

Composed by
Keele University Press
and printed by Hartnolls
in Bodmin, England

ISBN 1 85331 169 3

Contents

Introduction   7

Bibliography   16

The Poems of Lady Mary Wroth   19

    Pamphilia to Amphilanthus   21

    Poems from *The Countess of Mountgomeries Urania*   127

    Poems from the Newberry Manuscript
    The Secound Part of The Countess of Montgomery's Urania   200

Index of First Lines   221

Introduction

Study me then, you who shall lovers be
At the next world, that is, at the next spring:
   For I am every dead thing,
    In whom love wrought new alchemy.
      For his art did express
A quintessence even from nothingness,
From dull privations, and lean emptiness
He ruined me, and I am re-begot
Of absence, darkness, death; things which are not.

The second verse of John Donne's 'Nocturnal upon St Lucy's Day' seems to sum up most powerfully and effectively the paradoxical experience of the poetry of Lady Mary Wroth, the most important English woman writer of the earlier seventeenth century. The first Englishwoman to publish her own Petrarchan love poetry and prose fiction, she is of interest not merely for those historical facts, but because of the quality of her poetry and her presentation of a feminine sensibility struggling for expression in the context of an intensely male-dominated literary and social culture. Relatively little-known at the time, and largely neglected since, her writing has only fairly recently been rediscovered and received extensive discussion and 'study', by 'lovers' and others.

Lady Mary Wroth was probably born on 18 October 1587, the first child of Robert Sidney, later Viscount de L'Isle and Earl of Leicester, and Barbara (née Gamage). Her grandfather, Sir Henry Sidney, was a loyal Protestant administrator for Queen Elizabeth, and Lord Deputy of Ireland. Her uncle, Sir Philip Sidney, was a celebrated Protestant hero and courtier, author of the sonnet sequence *Astrophel and Stella* and the prose romance *The Countess of Pembroke's Arcadia,* and her aunt, Mary, Countess of Pembroke, was also a noted literary patron, translator (with Philip) of the Psalms and of other writing, and mother of William Herbert, third Earl of Pembroke. Her father was chiefly a career courtier and government servant, but also wrote poetry, and her mother was a literary patron. The title-page of Lady Mary's own published work, *The Countesse of Mountgomeries Urania*, ostentatiously parades her distinguished cultural and family pedigree: 'Daughter to the right Noble Robert Earle of Leicester. And Neece to the ever famous, and renowned Sir Phillips Sidney knight. And to the most exelent Lady Mary Countesse of Pembroke late deceased.'

As a child, she lived mostly in the family home, Penshurst Place, in northern Kent (celebrated in Ben Jonson's poem, 'To Penshurst'), visiting her (frequently absent, though fond) father in the Netherlands, where he was military governor, and London, where the family stayed at the Earl of Pembroke's London home, Baynard's Castle. She was brought to Elizabeth's court and, on 27 September 1604, was (as Jonson later put it) 'unworthily married to a jealous husband', Sir Robert Wroth; ten years her senior, he was the eldest son of a wealthy landowner, with estates in Loughton and Durrance in Essex that provided good hunting for King James (as noted in Jonson's 'To Sir Robert Wroth'). The marriage did not begin well: shortly after the wedding, Robert Sidney referred in a letter to 'words of grief', and to Robert Wroth's 'discontent', though the husband, he said, 'protests that he cannot take any exceptions to his wife, nor her carriage towards him'.

During the marriage, Lady Mary spent much time in London at Baynard's Castle and at court, where she became part of Queen Anne's entourage, though, as Jonson noted in his poem, her husband preferred country residence and hunting to court masques. Lady Mary herself took part in two of Jonson's court masques, *The Masque of Blackness* in 1605 (shortly after the court performance of *Othello*), for which she 'blacked-up' as a 'daughter of Niger', and *The Masque of Beauty* three years later. There appear to have been close connections between her and Jonson (who made a point of keeping in with the Sidneys and the Pembrokes), who dedicated his play *The Alchemist* to her in 1610 and wrote complimentary poems about her and her poetry ('I that have been a lover …'). It is remarkable that it was not until February 1614 that she bore her first child, James. A month later her husband died, leaving her with an annual jointure of £1,200, a month-old son and debts of £23,000. She attempted to deal with matters herself, but the son died in July 1616, whereupon the estate passed to Robert's brother and she was left with mounting debts. (She claimed to have paid off half the debt by 1624, but she was never free of financial difficulties.)

The early years of her widowhood were not concerned solely with financial matters. It appears that she had an adulterous relationship

8

(perhaps begun before her husband's death) with her first cousin, William Herbert, Earl of Pembroke (1580–1630). He also had married (probably for money) in 1604, shortly before her, and had established a reputation as an energetic courtier, active in court tilting-matches and politics, and something of a 'ladies' man' (as well as being a patron of Jonson and a minor poet himself). It is possible that an emotionally significant relationship had developed in the cousins' youth; they saw a lot of each other during her marriage; and, after her husband's death, she bore him two children, William and Catherine. How long the relationship lasted is not known.

The relationship was no secret and was apparently accepted by the Sidney and Pembroke families; such affairs were not uncommon and, if not too brazen, were frequently condoned at the Jacobean court. Nevertheless, Lady Mary fell into disfavour at court, either because of this or because of the publication, in 1621, of the *Urania,* dedicated to her friend and Pembroke's sister-in-law, Susan, Countess of Montgomery. It is not certain that she intended its publication (it could have brought her no money): despite the splendid title-page, there are no dedicatory poems or prefatory material, as was usual. She told the Duke of Buckingham that her writings 'from the first were solde against my minde, I never purposing to have had them published' (Roberts, p. 236), though she had in fact already presented him with a copy. Her sexual reputation was not good; worse, she had offended conventional expectations of women by writing non-religious material and by publishing; furthermore, the romance contained characters and episodes which were clearly based on real events and people, known at court, causing considerable scandal and forcing her to recall the books and to go into some degree of retirement. Thereafter she largely disappears from record, though presumably she continued writing for her own satisfaction (the second part of *Urania* and a pastoral play, *Love's Victorie*). It is thought that she died in about 1653.

Urania, the full title of which deliberately echoes Philip's *The Countess of Pembroke's Arcadia* (a new edition of which had appeared in 1621), is an enormous, rambling, unfinished chivalric romance in prose, of nearly 590,000 words in its two sections, the first printed incomplete, the other left incomplete in manuscript. It also contains some seventy-four poems and, at the end of the 1621 volume, a sonnet sequence of 103 lyrics, ostensibly by one of the characters, entitled *Pamphilia to Amphilanthus*. A brief account of some elements of *Urania* may be helpful as background to the poetry.

The story is set in a fantasy Greece and eastern Europe, with many interlaced narratives concerning the amours, escapades and conflicts of numerous kings, queens, princes, princesses, knights and ladies, sometimes disguised as shepherds and shepherdesses, together with various brigands, magicians, giants and so on. Episodes and characters, ringing variations on a few themes of faithful and unfaithful love, jealousy, endurance and melancholy, derive not only from others' lives but her own: Pamphilia ('all-loving'), the chief female character, is a figure for Wroth herself, and Amphilanthus ('lover of two') may reasonably be linked with William Herbert; their story provides much of what structure the story has. Amphilanthus, Prince of Naples, is initially in love with Antissia, Princess of Romania, while Princess (later Queen) Pamphilia, his first cousin, conceals her love for him; they eventually declare their love for each other. When Rodomandro, King of Tartaria, falls in love with Pamphilia, Amphilanthus asks her to marry him, which she does, though the contract is not legally binding. Later, Amphilanthus is deliberately misinformed that she has married Rodomandro, and marries the Princess of Slavonia. The King of Tartaria defends Pamphilia against the Sophie of Persia and, encouraged by her father, she marries him, though still in love with Amphilanthus. Later, the King dies, leaving her with a son who also dies soon; she and Amphilanthus meet again and are partially reconciled.

Lady Mary figures in the stories of other women characters. Bellamira (beautiful Mari) and her beloved are misinformed that each is betrothed to another, so she accepts her father's choice, Treborius (Robert), who loves hunting; he dies, as does their son soon after, and she retires from court. Lindamira, eldest daughter of Bersindor (Robert Sidney), is much favoured by the Queen of France (England); she secretly loves someone also loved by the Queen (or Queen Mother) who, as a result of malicious gossip, turns against her and exiles her from court. There are also Lisia – forced by her parents to marry 'so dull a piece of flesh, as this or any country need know' – Limena – who, despite loving another, marries her father's choice, a jealous, domineering man – and Lady Pastora – who, though married, has an adulterous relationship with her married lover. Mary Lamb summarizes much of the book neatly: 'Various narratives about women married against their will gradually yield to narratives about the happiness of second loves, which gradually yield to narratives about sad constant heroines whose beloveds leave them for yet a second time' (Lamb, p.145) — which perhaps tells us something of Wroth's story of her life and provides the context in which the poems originally appeared.

Whenever Wroth wrote her sonnets (and some at least probably precede her husband's death), she was already old-fashioned and belated in using that form. Philip had written his sonnet sequence in the early 1580s and the sonnet craze of the 1590s was long exhausted when she started writing. She was always more a member of the Sidney family than of the Wroths, and Philip's, Robert's and (in some ways, most of all) Mary's examples, as writers within a sophisticated court culture, must have given her confidence, though also producing various anxieties — about the presumptuousness of appearing to attempt to match that generation, of attempting to write as a woman, and especially of producing original writing in secular modes, which not even her distinguished aunt had attempted. Nevertheless, her writing clearly looks back to theirs and their evocations of a culture now increasingly under strain, while developing her own emphases and particular concerns.

Pamphilia to Amphilanthus exists in two forms, a manuscript (Folger MS v.a. 104) and the printed version of 1621. The former is presumably earlier, containing 110 lyrics, while 1621 contains 103, slightly differently arranged, with a few different poems and with more conventional punctuation and spelling. The order in the manuscript is as follows (see Roberts, p.64, who also prints the six Folger poems not in 1621): P1–3, Folger 1, P5–16, P64, P68, P70, P20–4, P72, P26–9, P65, P31–9, P95, P97, P42–6, P96, P48–55, Blank, P65–7, U18, P58–61, U14, P62, U12, P63, P17, P30, P66–7, P18, P69, P19, P71, P25, P73, F2, P74–5, U13, P76, P77–90, Blank, F3, P91–3, U34, P94, P40, P47, P41, P98–103, U32, F4–5, Blank, U52, F6, U17, U24. Each version begins with fifty-five poems, so ordered that eight sequences of six sonnets are each followed by a song, except for the last. In the 1621 text, the first sequence of forty-eight sonnets and seven songs is followed by several smaller sections: a sonnet and six songs, each headed 'sonnet' or 'song'; ten numbered sonnets and three songs; a sonnet introducing a corona or 'crown' of fourteen numbered, linked sonnets; four numbered songs; and nine numbered sonnets (forty-eight lyrics in all).

Like Philip and Robert, whose work she read with care, Wroth used the Italianate sonnet structure of separately rhymed octave and sestet, her most common rhyme schemes being *abbaabbaccdeed* (27) and *ababbabacdcdee* (17), followed by *ababbabaccdeed* (10), *ababbabacddcee* (8) and *abbaabbacddcee* (6); overall, both parts of *Urania* use twenty-three different rhyme patterns for the sonnets, including monorhyme. Clearly unafraid of technical experiment, Lady Mary also produced a corona of fourteen sonnets (P77–90), a form whereby the last line of each poem is repeated as the first of the next, with the very last repeating the very first, closing the circle (or, in this case, the labyrinth). Philip had composed a corona (of dizains) in the 'Old' *Arcadia* (*OA* 72), and Samuel Daniel and Donne had composed sonnet coronas, though Robert had failed to complete his; each sonnet really should be grammatically self-contained, but Wroth did not manage that.

In fact, she often has difficulty with her grammar; her sentences frequently lose direction, impetus and clarity, while nouns and verbs do not always agree in the way a modern reader would expect. The exigencies of rhyme and rhythm sometimes lead to over-compression and awkward inversion of word-order, and sometimes syllable-counting replaces proper rhythm. Nevertheless, there is an effective plainness of diction, graceful flow, and use of relatively straightforward 'conceits' or analogies, suggesting the general influence of Jonson, while colloquial directness and even vigour produce some well-phrased openings and final couplets; certainly, the simplicity and economy of which she is capable produce some moving effects.

The dominant imagery is of sun and fire, night and dark, clouds, stars and eyes, and hearts, with personifications of love as Venus and Cupid, and personifications of emotions such as grief, jealousy, hope and fear and some dominating conditions, particularly constancy, absence and silence — in fact, most of the familiar materials of Petrarchan verse.

Even if Wroth comes at the end of the sonnet vogue and towards the end of Petrarchism, she inevitably wears her rue with a singular difference, that of a woman writer, having to work with, or, rather, against, powerful and long-established literary and cultural forces. Petrarchism had long been the dominant codification (for men) of sexual love, though latterly it was increasingly undermined by more sceptical attitudes. In this, love is seen as intensely idealistic and inspiring (sometimes blending into Neoplatonism), but also frustrating; the (male) lover is caught in inner conflict, enflamed by desire and frozen by the despair provoked by the beloved's lack of response or inaccessibility. Paradox is the dominant rhetorical technique, painful self-contradiction the dominant state, as the lover incessantly pursues, yet denies himself, submits, yet seeks to manipulate. He may, almost fetishistically, blazon the lady's beauties or other qualities, but his main concern is with himself and his own exquisite agonies (idealism and masochism seem closely integrated here). In effect, he and his poetry depend upon her denial and absence for his self-exploration and self-creation (little, if anything, is heard from the beloved object, controlled and silenced as she is by social and literary convention). Petrarchist poetry, for all its (frequent) stylistic verve, seems characterized by an almost morbid introversion, obsessiveness, self-consciousness and sense of psychological instability.

Much of this applies to Lady Mary's poetry, but it is profoundly modified, chiefly as a result of the reversal of the gender role. Notably, the man is silenced, removed from sight (no blazonings for him) and, apart from a few sonnets to his eyes, not even addressed; except for possible puns on 'will' — for William Herbert — his identity is not suggested. The social and material world, so effectively evoked by Philip, is hardly present — one learns only of enclosed rooms, watching eyes, labyrinths, of 'molestation' from within and without; the focus is entirely on the solitary, withdrawn speaker and her obsessions and anxieties. The conventional requirement of chaste self-restraint which makes the beloved woman so negative also negates her as a lover (unable to pursue, or to express desire). Such attitudes are not looked for in the man, for whom the conventional 'coldness' of the love-object must be replaced by inaccessibility, either as a result of being already married (which cannot be made explicit), or absent, or (for literary purposes, the most effective) unfaithful and unreliable. The Petrarchan lover is always dependent on, and even shaped by, the other, the woman lover even more so, oscillating between hope and melancholic loss of self-esteem. Constancy in love was the normal requirement for women; here, the woman commits herself to it absolutely, almost neurotically, as the only stabilizing force, in the belief that whatever the man or Fortune may do, she will have this fixity, this (Stoic) virtue, this defining feature (the compulsive repetitiveness and masochism in Petrarchism seem particularly apparent). The quest for reciprocated love is a quest for an identity provided by another as well as a self-sufficient identifying force in itself; lack of response also produces a curious, negative identity. As with all Petrarchan lover-poets, the beloved's (necessary) absence is, paradoxically, a psychological presence (Philip's Astrophel speaks of 'absent presence' (*AS* 106)) and transforming force. The speaker is, she says, 'possessed' by the 'spirit, Absence', that has taken over her 'self' (P52). She falls silent; she effectively becomes Absence, Negation, in a self-denying self-affirmation, defined by that which is not there, 'things which are not'. Astrophel and other Petrarchan lover-poets preferred silence to verbiage; she also withdraws from the world, to interior dialogues with personified emotions which act out and define her desires in her inner self, the only world where, as woman and lover, she has autonomy. In poem after poem she welcomes and identifies with Night, in an inversion of values surpassing Shakespearean 'Dark Lady' inversions, in a condition expressed most powerfully in Donne's 'Nocturnal'.

In one sonnet, one of the few in this claustrophobic sequence to be even ostensibly directed outside herself, she claims insane possession (or dispossession): 'Alas, I am possessed, / And mad folks senseless are of wisdom' (P52); in *Urania* one of her unhappy poet-lover doubles, Antissia, is also mentally disturbed, regarding 'poetry ... in the perfection [as] but a delightful frenzy ... [and] poetical fury ... [as] in the true sense ... distraction'. Certainly, much of the poetry confronts a profound disordering of the sense of self as well as a sturdy engagement with that disorder; though 'led by the power of grief', not all of it is only 'to wailings brought' (P9). To some extent, self-fictionalization in *Urania* generally, and in *Pamphilia* particularly, must have served as a kind of therapy (which is why *Urania* could never have been completed, only abandoned).

In *Urania* generally, the poems are framed and contextually limited by their narrative context; to some extent, this is true of *Pamphilia to Amphilanthus,* altered as it is from the manuscript. Within it, one can also construct narratives, rather as can be done with Sidney's, Spenser's and Shakespeare's sonnet sequences — though they are, as it were, only gestures at narrative, being organized on other principles, as thematic analyses and explorations. In *Pamphilia to Amphilanthus* one can trace the (familiar) topics of the initial suffering of love, poems on writing love poetry, commitment to love and sorrow, poems on dreams, night, absence, rivals, jealousy, guilt and time; a major feature is provided by conflicting conceptions of love, figured as Venus and Cupid in shifting roles, variously seen as destructive, playful, or, in almost Neoplatonic fashion, as benign rulers and deities. The tone can be light, as in some of the songs which successfully evoke Elizabethan lyric, but it is usually sombre; the sequence ends with a recognition of the impossibility of temporal satisfaction and apparent 'calm of mind, all passion spent'. That, however, is not how the manuscript concludes; there the last poem is by Antissia, still unsatisfied: 'I who do feel the highest part of grief, / Shall I be left without relief?' (U24). One would like to think that the calm of 1621's conclusion is what the author felt; but it may well have been, like so much love poetry, only a self-serving fiction: 'lines … Increase the pain; grief is not cured by art' (P9).

A Note on the Text

This edition is based on the 1621 printed edition of *Urania* and the Newberry MS continuation. I have also consulted Gary Waller's edition of *Pamphilia to Amphilanthus* and the edition of the poems by Josephine Roberts which uses the Folger MS of *Pamphilia to Amphilanthus* but reorders that sequence according to 1621. Wroth's spelling is of much the same standard as most of her contemporaries', and spelling, orthography, etc. have been modernized in the usual way; where her spelling produces ambivalent readings, I have noted the original. Where a final '-ed' should be sounded for the sake of rhythm, this has been indicated thus: 'èd'; where rhythm requires the elision of a syllable, this is indicated by an apostrophe for the missing vowel. As the MSS indicate, Wroth's grammar, sentence construction and punctuation were relatively loose, frequently producing obscurity and uncertainty in interpretation (without this necessarily being intended or advantageous). The ordering of *Pamphilia to Amphilanthus* for the 1621 printing must be Wroth's: it seems probable that someone else made that edition more orthodox as regards spelling and punctuation, without solving all the problems, and it should not be thought of as having determining authority in every respect. In the belief that there is no virtue in unnecessary obscurity, and with a view to a modern – and particularly student – readership, punctuation has therefore been modified in several instances, with some caution, to clarify meaning.

Poems from the Newberry MS are reproduced by courtesy of the Newberry Library, Chicago.

Annotation

The following abbreviations have been used:

AS Sir Philip Sidney's *Astrophel and Stella*
OA Sir Philip Sidney's 'Old *Arcadia*', the first version of *The Countess of Pembroke's Arcadia*
RS 'The Poems of Robert Sidney'; the numbering is that of Katherine Duncan-Jones

Bibliography

Primary works

Published editions
Roberts, Josephine A., ed., *The Poems of Lady Mary Wroth* (Baton Rouge: Louisiana State University Press, 1983).
Waller, Gary, ed., *Pamphilia to Amphilanthus* (Salzburg: Universität Salzburg, 1977).
Wroth, Mary, *The Countesse of Mountgomeries Urania* (London: John Marriott and John Grismand, 1621).

Manuscripts
The Secound Part of the Countess of Montgomerys Urania, Newberry Library Case MS fY 1565. W95.
Sonnets and Songs, Folger MS v.a. 104.

Secondary works

Beilin, Elaine, ' "The Onely Perfect Vertue": Constancy in Lady Mary Wroth's *Pamphilia to Amphilanthus*', *Spenser Studies* II (1981), 229–45.
—— *Redeeming Eve: Women Writers in the Renaissance* (Princeton: Princeton University Press, 1987).
Croft, Peter, ed., *The Poems of Robert Sidney* (Oxford: Clarendon, 1984).
Donaldson, Ian, ed., *Ben Jonson* (Oxford and New York: Oxford University Press, 1985).
Duncan-Jones, Katherine, ed., 'The Poems of Robert Sidney', *English* XXX (1981) 136, 3–72.
Jones, Ann Rosalind, *The Currency of Eros: Women's Love Lyric in Europe, 1540–1620* (Bloomington: Indiana University Press, 1990).
Lamb, Mary Ellen, *Gender and Authorship in the Sidney Circle* (Madison: University of Wisconsin Press, 1990).

Miller, Naomi J., 'Rewriting Lyric Fictions: The Role of the Lady in Lady Mary Wroth's *Pamphilia to Amphilanthus*', in Haselkorn, Anne M., and Betty S. Travitsky, eds., *The Renaissance Englishwoman in Print: Counterbalancing the Canon* (Amherst: University of Massachusetts Press, 1990), 295–310.

Miller, Naomi J., and Gary Waller, eds., *Reading Mary Wroth. Representing Alternatives in Early Modern England* (Knoxville: University of Tennessee Press, 1991).

Paulissen, Mary Nelson, *The Love Sonnets of Lady Mary Wroth. A Critical Introduction* (Salzburg: Universität Salzburg, 1982).

Quilligan, Maureen, 'The Constant Subject: Instability and Female Authority in Wroth's *Urania* Poems', in Harvey, Elizabeth D., and Katherine Eisaman Maus, eds., *Soliciting Interpretation: Literary Theory and Seventeenth-Century English Poetry* (Chicago: University of Chicago Press, 1990), 303–36.

Ringler, William A., ed., *The Poems of Sir Philip Sidney* (Oxford: Clarendon, 1990).

Smith, A.J., ed., *John Donne. The Complete English Poems* (Harmondsworth: Penguin, 1971).

Wall, Wendy, *The Imprint of Gender. Authorship and Publication in the English Renaissance* (Ithaca and London: Cornell University Press, 1993).

Waller, Gary, *The Sidney Family Romance* (Detroit: Wayne State University Press, 1993).

Lady Mary Wroth with an Archlute, artist unknown (from the collection of Viscount De L'Isle, VC, KG, at Penshurst Place, Tonbridge, Kent).

LADY MARY WROTH
POEMS

A MODERNIZED EDITION

PAMPHILIA TO AMPHILANTHUS

[P1]   1.

When night's black mantle could most darkness prove,[1]
    And sleep, death's image, did my senses hire
    From knowledge of myself, then thoughts did move[2]
    Swifter than those, most swiftness need require.

In sleep, a chariot drawn by winged desire[3]   5
    I saw, where sat bright Venus, Queen of Love,
    And at her feet her son, still adding fire
    To burning hearts, which she did hold above;[4]

But one heart flaming more than all the rest[5]
    The goddess held, and put it to my breast.   10
    'Dear son, now shoot,'[6] said she, 'Thus must we win.'

He her obeyed, and martyred my poor heart.
    I, waking, hoped as dreams it would depart;
    Yet since, O me, a lover I have been.[7]

---

1. When night showed itself at its darkest.
2. When sleep temporarily engaged my senses, inducing unconsciousness (or lack of self-awareness).
3. See Shakespeare, *Hamlet*, I. v. 29–30: 'wings as swift / As meditation or the thoughts of love'.
4. The dream vision of the triumphal ride of Venus derives ultimately from Petrarch's *Trionfe d'Amore*. See also *AS* 79. 4: 'Which, coupling doves, guides Venus' chariot right', and Jonson, *Celebration of Charis*: 'See the chariot at hand here of Love'.
5. Venus holds a flaming heart in *Urania*, as depicted on the title page. In Dante's *Vita Nuova* III he sees Love feeding Dante's own burning heart to his beloved, Beatrice.
6. shoot] MS reads 'shutt'; 'shut' produces a possible, but difficult, reading, whereby Cupid locks up the dreamer's heart; he is usually associated with shooting arrows of love.
7. been] Pronounced (and spelt in MS) 'bin'.

Dear eyes, how well, indeed, you do adorn
    That blessèd sphere which gazing souls hold dear,
    The lovèd place of sought-for triumphs, near
    The court of glory,[1] where love's force was born.

How may they term you April's sweetest morn,   5
    When pleasing looks from those bright lights appear,
    A sun-shine day; from clouds and mists still clear,
    Kind nursing fires for wishes yet unborn!

Two stars of heaven,[2] sent down to grace the earth,
    Placed in that throne which gives all joys their birth,   10
    Shining and burning, pleasing yet their charms,

Which, wounding, ev'n in hurts are deemed delights,
    So pleasant is their force, so great their mights
    As, happy, they can triumph in their harms.

---

1. 1621 capitalizes 'Court' and 'Glory'; if significant at all, it could suggest the court of Queen Elizabeth, or Gloriana, where Mary could have met William Herbert before his temporary banishment from court in 1601; she often visited his London home, Baynard's Castle, near the court, both before and after her marriage.
2. The eyes–stars comparison is conventional. *RS* uses it frequently. See also Shakespeare, *Romeo and Juliet*, II. ii. 15–17: 'Two of the fairest stars in all the heaven, / Having some business, do entreat her eyes / To twinkle in their spheres till they return'.

Yet is there hope. Then, Love, but play thy part,
   Remember well thyself, and think on me;
   Shine in those eyes which conquered have my heart,[1]
   And see if mine be slack to answer thee.

Lodge in that breast, and pity moving see   5
   For flames which in mine burn in truest smart,[2]
   Exiling thoughts that touch inconstancy,
   Or those which waste not in the constant art.

Watch but my sleep, if I take any rest
   For thought of you, my spirit so distressed   10
   As, pale and famished, I for mercy cry.[3]

Will you your servant leave? Think but on this:
   Who wears love's crown must not do so amiss,
   But seek their good, who on thy force do lie.[4]

---

1. See *AS* 12. 1: 'Cupid, because thou shinest in Stella's eyes'.
2. There see pity for flames which burn in truest smart in my breast.
3. See whether I take any rest as a result of thinking of you, my spirit being so distressed that, pale and famished, I cry for mercy.
4. lie] Rely.

Forbear, dark night, my joys now bud again,[1]
    Lately grown dead, while cold aspects did chill
    The root at heart, and my chief hope quite kill,
    And thunders struck me in my pleasure's wane.

Then I, alas, with bitter sobs and pain   5
    Privately groaned my fortune's present ill;
    All light of comfort dimmed, woe in prides[2] fill,
    With strange increase of grief I grieved in vain.

And most, as when a memory to good
    Molested me, which still as witness stood   10
    Of these best days in former times I knew,

Late gone, as wonders past, like the great Snow,[3]
    Melted and wasted, with what change must know:
    Now back the life comes where as once it grew.

---

1.   For the metaphor of the reviving plant, see also George Herbert's 'The Flower'.
2.   Woes replaced pride.
3.   Snow] Capitalized, presumably referring to some particularly severe snow-fall, perhaps that referred to by Thomas Dekker in *The Cold Year, 1614, a Deep Snow* (1615).

Can pleasing sight misfortune ever bring?
   Can firm desire a painful torment try?
   Can winning eyes prove to the heart a sting?
   Or can sweet lips in treason hidden lie?

The sun, most pleasing, blinds the strongest eye   5
   If too much looked on, breaking the sight's string; [1]
   Desires still crossed must unto mischief hie,
   And as despair a luckless chance may fling. [2]

Eyes, having won, rejecting proves a sting,
   Killing the bud before the tree doth spring;   10
   Sweet lips, not loving, do as poison prove.

Desire, sight, eyes, lips, seek, see, prove and find, [3]
   You love may win, but curses if unkind:
   Then show you harms dislike, and joy in love.

---

1.   The eyes were thought to emit invisible beams, thus enabling sight; see Donne, 'The Extasie': 'our eye-beams twisted, and did thread / Our eyes upon one double string'.
2.   Some people provoke but thwart desire, turning to harm, and unfortunately producing despair in their lovers.
3.   This cumulative rhetorical pattern was popular in the late sixteenth century; see *AS* 100, and Kyd's *The Spanish Tragedy* (1589?), III. ii. 1–24, esp. 22–4: 'Eyes, life, world, heavens, hell, night and day, / See, search, show, send, some man, / Some mean, that may —'.

O strive not still to heap disdain on me,
    Nor pleasure take, your cruelty to show
    On hapless me, on whom all sorrows flow,
    And biding make, as given and lost by thee.

Alas, ev'n grief is grown to pity me;   5
    Scorn cries out 'gainst itself such ill to show,
    And would give place for joy's delights to flow;
    Yet wretched I all tortures bear from thee.

Long have I suffered, and esteemed it dear,
    Since such thy will, yet grew my pain more near.   10
    Wish you my end? Say so, you shall it have,

For all the depth of my heart-held despair
    Is that for you I feel not death for care;
    But now I'll seek it, since you will not save.

Song. 1.

'The spring now come at last
   To trees, fields, to flowers
And meadows makes to taste
   His pride, while sad showers
Which from mine eyes do flow,   5
   Makes known with cruel pains
   Cold winter yet remains,
No sign of spring we know.

'The sun which to the earth
   Gives heat, light and pleasure,   10
Joys in spring, hateth dearth,
   Plenty makes his treasure.
His heat to me is cold,
   His light all darkness is,
   Since I am barred of bliss   15
I heat nor light behold.'

A shepherdess thus said,[1]
   Who was with grief oppressed,
For truest love betrayed
   Barred her from quiet rest;   20
And weeping, thus said she:
   'My end approacheth near,
   Now willow[2] must I wear,
My fortune so will be.

'With branches of this tree   25
   I'll dress my hapless head,
Which shall my witness be
   My hopes in love are dead;
My clothes embroidered all
   Shall be with garlands round,   30
   Some scattered, others bound,
Some tied, some like to fall.

---

1. See *RS* Song 3. 63ff.: 'Thus said a shepherd, once / With weights of change oppressed, / For he had lost at once / What ever he loved best …'.
2. The willow is a conventional symbol of disappointed love; see *Othello*, II. iii. 39.

The bark[1] my book shall be,
 Where daily I will write
This tale of hapless me,   35
 True slave to fortune's spite;
The root[1] shall be my bed,
 Where nightly I will lie
 Wailing inconstancy,
Since all true love is dead.   40

'And these lines I will leave,
 If some such lover come
Who may them right conceive,
 And place them on my tomb:
She who still constant loved,   45
 Now dead with cruel care,
 Killed with unkind despair
And change, her end here proved.'

---

1. bark, root] See U5 and U6.

Love, leave to urge, thou know'st thou hast the hand;
   'Tis cowardice to strive where none resist;
   Pray thee leave off, I yield unto thy band;
   Do not thus still in thine own power persist.

Behold, I yield; let forces be dismissed;   5
   I am thy subject, conquered, bound to stand;
   Never thy foe, but did thy claim assist,
   Seeking thy due of those who did withstand.

But now, it seems, thou would'st I should thee love.
   I do confess, 'twas thy will made me choose,   10
   And thy fair shows made me a lover prove,
   When I my freedom did for pain refuse.

Yet this, Sir God, your boyship I despise;
Your charms I obey, but love not want of eyes.[1]

---

1. Blind Cupid was a symbol of the irrationality of love; see Shakespeare, *A Midsummer Night's Dream*, I. i. 234–7.

Led by the pow'r of grief, to wailings brought
　　By false conceit of change fall'n on my part,[1]
　　I seek for some small ease by lines which, bought,
　　Increase the pain; grief is not cured by art.

Ah! how unkindness moves within the heart   5
　　Which still is true and free from changing thought;
　　What unknown woe it breeds, what endless smart,
　　With ceaseless tears which causelessly are wrought.

It makes me now to shun all shining light,
　　And seek for blackest clouds me light to give,   10
　　Which to all others only darkness drive;
　　They on me shine, for sun disdains my sight.

Yet though I dark do live, I triumph may:
Unkindness nor this wrong shall love allay.

1.　Falsely suspected of infidelity.

Be you all pleased? Your pleasures grieve not me.
 Do you delight? I envy not your joy.
 Have you content? Contentment with you be.
 Hope you for bliss? Hope still, and still enjoy.

Let sad misfortune hapless me destroy,   5
 Leave crosses[1] to rule me, and still rule free,
 While all delights their contraries employ
 To keep good back, and I but torments see.

Joys are bereaved, harms do only tarry,
 Despair takes place, disdain hath got the hand; 10
 Yet firm love holds my senses in such band
 As, since despised, I with sorrow marry.

Then if with grief I now must coupled be,
Sorrow I'll wed:[2] despair thus governs me.

---

1. crosses] Misfortunes, afflictions.
2. See *AS* 100. 14: 'All mirth farewell, let me in sorrow live', and *RS* 7. 9–10:
 'Divorced from pleasures, marry / Henceforth we do with care'.

The weary traveller who, tired, sought
   In places distant far, yet found no end
   Of pain or labour, nor his state to mend,
   At last with joy is to his home back brought,

Finds not more ease, though he with joy be fraught,   5
   When past is fear, content like souls ascend,[1]
   Than I, on whom new pleasures do descend,
   Which now as high as first-born bliss is wrought.

He, tired with his pains, I with my mind;
   He all content receives by ease of limbs,   10
   I, greatest happiness that I do find
   Belief for faith, while hope in pleasure swims.

Truth saith, 'twas wrong conceit bred my despite,[2]
Which, once acknowledged, brings my heart's delight.

---

1. When fear is past, the feeling of contentment rises, like souls to heaven.
2. She was misunderstood, which caused her mistreatment.

You endless torments that my rest oppress,
    How long will you delight in my sad pain?
    Will never love your favour more express?
    Shall I still live, and ever feel disdain?

Alas, now stay, and let my grief obtain   5
    Some end; feed not my heart with sharp distress;
    Let me once see my cruel fortunes gain
    At least release, and long-felt woes redress.

Let not the blame of cruelty disgrace
    The honoured title of your godhead, Love;   10
    Give not just cause for me to say, a place
    Is found for rage alone on me to move.

O quickly end, and do not long debate
My needful aid, lest help do come too late.

Cloyed with the torments of a tedious night,
   I wish for day; which come, I hope for joy;
   When cross I find new tortures to destroy
   My woe-killed heart, first hurt by mischief's might;[1]

Then cry for night, and once more day takes flight.   5
   And brightness gone, what rest should here enjoy
   Usurpèd is: Hate will her force employ;
   Night cannot Grief entomb, though black as spite.

My thoughts are sad, her face[2] as sad doth seem;
   My pains are long, her hours tedious are;   10
   My grief is great, and endless is my care;
   Her face, her force, and all of woes esteem.

Then welcome Night, and farewell flatt'ring day,
Which all hopes breed, and yet our joys delay.[3]

---

1. See also *AS* 89.
2. her face] Night's.
3. See Surrey, 'The soote season ...': 'Each care decays, and yet my sorrow springs'.

All night I weep, all day I cry, ay me,
I still do wish, though yet deny, ay me;
I sigh, I mourn, I say that still
I only am the store for ill, ay me.[1]

In coldest hopes I freeze, yet burn, ay me,   5
From flames I strive to fly, yet turn, ay me;
From grief I haste, but sorrows hie,
And on my heart all woes do lie, ay me.

From contraries[2] I seek to run, ay me,
But contraries I cannot shun, ay me: 10
For they delight their force to try,
And to despair my thoughts do tie, ay me.

Whither, alas, then shall I go, ay me,
When as despair all hopes outgo, ay me?
If to the forest, Cupid hies,   15
And my poor soul to his laws ties, ay me.

To the Court? O no, he cries, ay me,[3]
There no true love you shall espy, ay me,
Leave that place to falsest lovers,
Your true love all truth discovers, ay me.   20

Then quiet rest, and no more prove, ay me;
All places are alike to love, ay me;
And constant be in this begun,
Yet say, till life with love be done, ay me.

---

1. ay me] By repetition, this could also suggest 'aye, me', for emphasis, or 'I, me', as the speaker identifies herself with constancy and grief.
2. These 'contraries' derive ultimately from Petrarch's *Rime* 134; see Wyatt, 'I find no peace and all my war is done. / I fear and hope, I burn and freeze like ice …'.
3. The presence of true love in the country, and absence from court, is a familiar topic; see Spenser, *Colin Clouts Come Home Againe*, 766–74.

Dear, famish not what you yourself gave food,
    Destroy not what your glory is to save,[1]
    Kill not that soul to which you spirit gave:
In pity, not disdain, your triumph stood.

An easy thing it is to shed the blood   5
    Of one who, at your will, yields to the grave,
    But more you may true worth[2] by mercy crave
When you preserve, not spoil but nourish good.

Your sight is all the food I do desire;
    Then sacrifice me not in hidden fire,   10
    Or stop the breath which did your praises move.

Think but how easy 'tis a sight to give,
    Nay, ev'n desert, since by it I do live;
    I but chameleon-like[3] would live, and love.

---

1.   See *RS* 26. 13–14: 'O save: do not destroy what is your own: / Just prince to spoil himself was never known'.
2.   worth] There may be a play on 'Wroth' (as in some other poems).
3.   The chameleon was popularly believed to live on air; see *Hamlet,* III. ii. 91–2: '… the chameleon's dish. I eat the air, promise-crammed'.

Am I thus conquered? Have I lost the powers
    That to withstand, which joys to ruin me?
    Must I be still, while it my strength devours,
    And captive leads me prisoner, bound, unfree?

Love first shall leave men's fancies to them free,   5
    Desire shall quench love's flames, Spring hate sweet showers,
    Love shall lose all his darts, have sight, and see
    His shame and wishings hinder happy hours.

Why should we not Love's purblind charms resist?
    Must we be servile, doing what he list?   10
    No, seek some host to harbour thee: I fly

Thy babish tricks, and freedom do profess.
    But O, my hurt makes my lost heart confess:
    I love, and must; so, farewell liberty.[1]

---

1.   The complaint of loss of liberty derives ultimately from Petrarch's *Rime* 97;
      see esp. *AS* 47, which has a similar final reversal.

Truly, poor Night, thou welcome art to me,
 I love thee better in this sad attire
 Than that which raiseth some men's fancies higher,
 Like painted outsides, which foul inward be.[1]

I love thy grave and saddest looks to see,   5
 Which seems my soul and dying heart entire,
 Like to the ashes of some happy fire
 That flamed in joy, but quenched in misery.

I love thy count'nance, and thy sober pace
 Which evenly goes, and as of loving grace   10
 To us, and me amongst the rest oppressed,

Gives quiet peace to my poor self alone,
 And freely grants day leave, when thou art gone,
 To give clear light to see all ill redressed.

---

1. See *AS* 96 and 97.

Sleep, fie, possess me not, nor do not fright[1]
    Me with thy heavy, and thy deathlike might:
    For counterfeiting's vilder[2] than death's sight,
    And such deluding more my thoughts do spite.

Thou suff'rest falsest shapes my soul t'affright,   5
    Sometimes in likeness of a hopeful sprite,
    And oft times like my love, as in despite,
    Joying thou canst with malice kill delight,

When I (a poor fool made by thee) think joy
    Doth flow, when thy fond shadows do destroy   10
    My that-while senseless self, left free to thee.

But now do well, let me for ever sleep,
    And so for ever that dear image keep,
    Or still wake, that my senses may be free.

---

1.   The poet's love dream and delusions is a topic going back to Petrarch at least
     and common in the Renaissance; see esp. *AS* 38.
2.   vilder] Viler.

Sweet shades, why do you seek to give delight
   To me, who deem delight in this vild¹ place
   But torment, sorrow, and mine own disgrace
   To taste of joy, or your vain pleasing sight?

Show them your pleasures who saw never night   5
   Of grief, where joying's fawning, smiling face
   Appears as day, where grief found never space
   Yet for a sigh, a groan, or envy's spite.

But O, on me a world of woes do lie,
   Or else on me all harms strive to rely,   10
   And to attend like servants bound to me.

Heat in desire, while frosts of care I prove,
   Wanting my love, yet surfeit do with love,
   Burn, and yet freeze: better in hell to be.

---

1. vild] Vile.

Which should I better like of, day or night?
  Since all the day I live in bitter woe,
  Enjoying light more clear, my wrongs to know,
  And yet most sad, feeling in it all spite.

In night, when darkness doth forbid all light   5
  Yet see I grief apparent to the show,
  Followed by jealousy, whose fond[1] tricks flow,
  And on unconstant waves of doubt alight.

I can behold rage[2] cowardly to feed
  Upon foul error, which these humours breed,   10
  Shame, doubt and fear, yet boldly will think ill.

All these in both I feel; then which is best,
  Dark to joy by day, light in night oppressed?
  Leave both, and end: these but each other spill.[3]

---

1. fond] foolish.
2. 'Rage' could mean, then, not only anger, but madness or lust.
3. spill] Kill or destroy.

Stay, my thoughts, do not aspire
   To vain hopes of high desire;
   See you not all means bereft
   To enjoy? No joy is left,
   Yet still methinks my thoughts do say,   5
   Some hopes do live amid dismay.

Hope, then once more, hope for joy,
   Bury fear which joys destroy;
   Thought hath yet some comfort giv'n,
   Which despair hath from us driv'n;   10
   Therefore dearly my thoughts cherish,
   Never let such thinking perish.

'Tis an idle thing to plain,
   Odder far to die for pain;
   Think, and see how thoughts do rise,   15
   Winning where there no hope lies,
   Which alone is lovers' treasure,
   For by thoughts we love do measure.

Then, kind thought, my fancy guide,
   Let me never hapless slide;   20
   Still maintain thy force in me,
   Let me thinking still be free,
   Nor leave thy might until my death,
   But let me thinking yield up breath.

Come darkest night, becoming sorrow best,[1]
    Light, leave thy light, fit for a lightsome soul:[2]
    Darkness doth truly suit with me oppressed,
    Whom absence' power doth from mirth control.[3]

The very trees with hanging heads condole   5
    Sweet summer's parting, and, of leaves distressed[4]
    In dying colours make a grief-full role,
    So much, alas, to sorrow are they pressed.

Thus of dead leaves her farewell carpet's made;
    Their fall, their branches, all their mournings prove,[5]   10
    With leafless, naked bodies, whose hues vade[6]
    From hopeful green, to wither in their love.

If trees and leaves, for absence, mourners be,
No marvel that I grieve, who like want see.

---

1. For this and the following sonnet, see *RS* 42 and 43.
2. See *RS* 42. 1–3: 'Absence, I cannot say thou hid'st my light, / Nor darkened, but for aye set is my sun; / No day sees me …'.
3. The power of sorrow at the beloved's absence prevents happiness.
4. The trees act out their sorrow for the parting of summer in costumes of dying leaves.
5. The fallen leaves and bare branches are revealed as the trees' act and garments of mourning. See *RS* 43. 1–2, 4–5: 'Forsaken woods, trees with sharp storms oppressed, / Whose leaves once hid the sun, now strew the ground … Gardens, which once in thousand colours dressed / Showed nature's pride'.
6. vade] Fade.

The sun which glads the earth at his bright sight,
   When in the morn he shows his golden face,
   And takes the place from tedious drowsy night,[1]
   Making the world still happy in his grace,

Shows happiness remains not in one place,   5
   Nor may the heavens alone to us give light,
   But hide that cheerful face, though no long space,
   Yet long enough for trial of their might.

But never sun-set could be so obscure,
   No desert[2] ever had a shade so sad,   10
   Nor could black darkness ever prove so bad
   As pains which absence makes me now endure.

The missing of the sun awhile makes night,
But absence of my joy sees never light.[3]

---

1.   The association of darkness and absence is conventional; see *AS* 89 and 91;
     but see note to previous sonnet, for echoes of *RS* 42, and 43.
2.   desert] Any uninhabited place.
3.   See *RS* 42. 1–3: 'Absence, I cannot say thou hid'st my light, / Not darkened,
     but for aye set is my sun; / No day sees me …'.

When last I saw thee, I did not thee see,[1]
    It was thine image, which in my thoughts lay
    So lively figured, as no time's delay
    Could suffer me in heart to parted be;

And sleep so favourable is to me,   5
    As not to let thy loved remembrance stray,
    Lest that I, waking, might have cause to say,
    There was one minute found to forget thee.

Then since my faith is such, so kind my sleep
    That gladly thee presents into my thought,   10
    And still true-lover-like thy face doth keep,
    So as some pleasure shadow-like is wrought:

Pity my loving, nay, of conscience, give
Reward to me, in whom thy self doth live.

---

1.   The love dream is a frequent Renaissance topic; see esp. *AS* 38.

Like to the Indians, scorchèd with the sun,
    The sun which they do as their god adore,
    So am I used by Love, for, ever more
    I worship him, less favours have I won.

Better are they who thus to blackness run,[1]   5
    And so can only whiteness' want deplore,
    Than I who pale and white am with grief's store,
    Nor can have hope, but to see hopes undone.

Besides, their sacrifice received's[2] in sight
    Of their chose saint, mine hid as worthless rite.   10
    Grant me to see where I my off'rings give,

Then let me wear the mark of Cupid's might
    In heart, as they in skin of Phoebus' light,[3]
    Not ceasing off'rings to Love while I live.

---

1. Lady Mary 'blacked-up' to take part in Jonson's *Masque of Blackness* in 1605.
2. received's] Received is.
3. Cf. Shakespeare, *Antony and Cleopatra*, I. v. 27–8: 'Think on me, / That am with Phoebus' amorous pinches black …'.

When every one to pleasing pastime hies,
    Some hunt,[1] some hawk, some play, while some delight
    In sweet discourse, and music shows joy's might;
    Yet I my thoughts do far above these prize.

The joy which I take is, that free from eyes   5
    I sit, and wonder at this day-like night,
    So to dispose themselves, as void of right,[2]
    And leave true pleasure for poor vanities.

If hawk, my mind at wishèd end doth fly;   10
    Discourse, I with my spirit talk, and cry
    While others music choose as greatest grace.

O God, say I, can these fond[3] pleasures move,
Or music be but in sweet thoughts of love?

---

1. Sir Robert Wroth was particularly keen on hunting; King James hunted on his estate.
2. Wonder at the blindness of those participating in such daytime activities, giving themselves up as though they had no choice.
3. fond] Foolish.

24.

Once did I hear an aged father say
    Unto his son, who with attention hears
    What age and wise experience ever clears
    From doubts of fear or reason to betray,

'My son,' said he, 'behold thy father gray;   5
    I once had, as thou hast, fresh tender years,
    And like thee sported, destitute of fears;
    But my young faults made me too soon decay.

'Love once I did, and like thee feared my love,
    Led by the hateful thread of jealousy: 10
    Striving to keep, I lost my liberty,
    And gained my grief, which still my sorrows move.

'In time shun this; to love is no offence,
But doubt in youth, in age breeds penitence.'

Sweetest love return again,
   Make not too long stay
Killing mirth and forcing pain,
   Sorrow leading way:
Let us not thus parted be,   5
Love and absence ne'er agree.[1]

But since you must needs depart,
   And me hapless leave,
In your journey take my heart,
   Which will not deceive: 10
Yours it is, to you it flies,
Joying in those lovèd eyes.

So in part we shall not part,
   Though we absent be;
Time nor place nor greatest smart   15
   Shall my bands make free:
Tied I am, yet think it gain;
In such knots I feel no pain.

But can I live, having lost
   Chiefest part of me?   20
Heart is fled, and sight is crossed:
   These my fortunes be.
Yet dear heart go, soon return:
As good there, as here to burn.

---

1.   See Donne's song, 'Sweetest love I do not go …'.

Poor eyes be blind, the light behold no more,
    Since that is gone which is your dear delight,
    Ravished from you by greater pow'r and might,
    Making your loss a gain to others' store.

O'erflow and drown, till sight to you restore   5
    That blessèd star, and, as in hateful spite,
    Send forth your tears in floods, to kill all sight
    And looks, that lost wherein you joyed before.

Bury these beams which in some kindled fires,
    And conquered have, their love-burnt hearts' desires   10
    Losing, and yet no gain by you esteemed;

Till that bright star do once again appear,
    Brighter than Mars when he doth shine most clear,
    See not; then by his might be you redeemed.

Dear, cherish this,[1] and with it my soul's will,[2]
    Nor for it ran away do it abuse:
    Alas, it left poor me, your breast to choose,
    As the blest shrine where it would harbour still.

Then favour show, and not unkindly kill   5
    The heart which fled to you, but do excuse
    That which for better, did the worse refuse,
    And pleased I'll be, though heartless my life spill.

But if you will be kind, and just indeed,
    Send me your heart, which in mine's place shall feed   10
    On faithful love to your devotion bound;

There shall it see the sacrifices made
    Of pure and spotless love which shall not vade
    While soul and body are together found.

---

1.   this] Heart. The exchange of lovers' hearts was a common topic; see esp. *Arcadia,* Book Three (*OA* 45): 'My true love hath my heart, and I have his …'.
2.   will] Possibly here, as elsewhere, a play on 'Will' (for William Herbert).

Fie, tedious Hope, why do you still rebel?
    Is it not yet enough you flattered me,[1]
    But cunningly you seek to use a spell
    How to betray; must these your trophies be?

I looked from you far sweeter fruit to see,   5
    But blasted were your blossoms when they fell,
    And those delights expected from hands free,
    Withered and dead, and what seemed bliss proves hell.

No town was won by a more plotted sleight
    Than I by you, who may my fortune write   10
    In embers of that fire which ruined me:

Thus, Hope, your falsehood calls you to be tried.
    You're loth, I see, the trial to abide;
    Prove true at last, and gain your liberty.

---

1.   See *AS* 67: 'Hope, art thou true, or dost thou flatter me?'

Grief,[1] killing grief, have not my torments been[2]
   Already great and strong enough, but still
   Thou dost increase, nay glory in, my ill,
   And woes new past, afresh new woes begin?

Am I the only purchase thou canst win?   5
   Was I ordained to give despair her fill,
   Or fittest I should mount misfortune's hill,
   Who in the plain of joy cannot live in?

If it be so, Grief come as welcome guest,
   Since I must suffer for another's rest;   10
   Yet this, good Grief, let me entreat of thee:

Use still thy force, but not from those I love
   Let me all pains and lasting torments prove;[3]
   So I miss these, lay all thy weights on me.

---

1. See *AS* 94, for a similar apostrophe of Grief, and final reversal.
2. been] Pronounced 'bin'.
3. Let me not experience pains and torments from those I love.

Fly hence, O Joy, no longer here abide:
　　Too great thy pleasures are for my despair
　　To look on; losses now must prove my fare
　　Who, not long since, on better fare relied.

But fool, how oft had I Heav'n's changing spied   5
　　Before of mine own fate I could have care,
　　Yet now, past time I can too late beware,
　　When nothing's left but sorrows faster tied.

While I enjoyed that sun whose sight did lend
　　Me joy, I thought that day could have no end: 10
　　But soon a night came clothed in absence dark,

Absence more sad, more bitter than is gall,
　　Or death when on true lovers it doth fall,
　　Whose fires of love, disdain rests poorer spark.[1]

1.　The fires of true love are covered over and suppressed by the worse fire of
　　disdain.

30.

You blessèd shades, which give me silent rest,
    Witness but this when death hath closed mine eyes,
    And separated me from earthly ties,
    Being from hence to higher place addressed,

How oft in you I have lain here oppressed,   5
    And have my miseries in woeful cries
    Delivered forth, mounting up to the skies
    Yet helpless back returned to wound my breast,

Which wounds did but strive how to breed more harm
    To me, who can be cured by no one charm   10
    But that of love, which yet may me relieve;

If not, let death my former pains redeem,
    My trusty friends, my faith untouched esteem,
    And witness I could love, who so could grieve.

Time, only cause of my unrest,
By whom I hoped once to be blessed,
   How cruel art thou turned,
That first gav'st life unto my love,
And still a pleasure not to move   5
   Or change, though ever burned;

Have I thee slacked, or left undone
One loving rite, and so have won
   Thy rage or bitter changing,
That now no minutes I shall see   10
Wherein I may least happy be,
   Thy favours so estranging?

Blame thy self and not my folly,
Time gave time but to be holy;
   True love such ends best loveth.   15
Unworthy love doth seek for ends,
A worthy love but worth pretends,
   Nor other thoughts it proveth.

Then stay thy swiftness, cruel Time,
And let me once more blessed climb   20
   To joy, that I may praise thee:
Let me, pleasure sweetly tasting,
Joy in love, and faith not wasting,
   And on Fame's wings I'll raise thee;

Never shall thy glory dying   25
Be until thine own untying,
   That Time no longer liveth;
'Tis a gain such time to lend,
Since so thy fame shall never end,
   But joy for what she giveth.   30

After long trouble in a tedious way
    Of love's unrest, laid down to ease my pain,
    Hoping for rest, new torments I did gain,
    Possessing me, as if I ought t'obey,

When Fortune came, though blinded, yet did stay,   5
    And in her blessèd arms did me enchain;
    I, cold with grief, thought no warmth to obtain,
    Or to dissolve that ice of joy's decay,

Till, 'Rise,' said she, 'Reward to thee doth send
    By me, the servant of true lovers, joy;   10
    Banish all clouds of doubt, all fears destroy,
    And now on Fortune, and on Love depend.'

I her obeyed, and rising felt that love
Indeed was best, when I did least it move.

32.

How fast thou fliest, O Time, on Love's swift wings,
 To hopes of joy, that flatters our desire,
 Which to a lover still contentment brings;
 Yet, when we should enjoy, thou dost retire.

Thou stay'st thy pace, false Time, from our desire,   5
 When to our ill thou hast'st with eagle's wings,
 Slow only to make us see thy retire
 Was for despair and harm, which sorrow brings.

O slack thy pace, and milder pass to Love,
 Be like the bee, whose wings she doth but use   10
 To bring home profit, master's good to prove,
 Laden and weary, yet again pursues.

So lade thy self with honey of sweet joy,
And do not me, the hive of love, destroy.

How many eyes, poor Love, hast thou to guard
   Thee from thy most desirèd wish and end?
   Is it because some say thou'rt blind that, barred
   From sight, thou should'st no happiness attend?

Who blame thee so, small justice can pretend,   5
   Since 'twixt thee and the sun no question hard
   Can be, his sight but outward, thou canst bend
   The heart, and guide it freely; thus, unbarred

Art thou, while we, both blind and bold, oft dare
   Accuse thee of the harms ourselves should find: 10
   Who, led with folly and by rashness blind,
   Thy sacred pow'r do with a child's compare.

Yet Love, this boldness pardon: for admire
Thee sure we must, or be born without fire.

Take heed mine eyes, how you your looks do cast,
　　Lest they betray my heart's most secret thought: [1]
　　Be true unto yourselves, for nothing's bought
　　More dear than doubt, which brings a lover's fast.

Catch you all watching eyes, ere they be past,   5
　　Or take yours, fixed where your best love hath sought
　　The pride of your desires; let them be taught
　　Their faults, for shame they could no truer last.

Then look, and look with joy, for conquest won
　　Of those that searched your hurt in double kind;   10
　　So you kept safe, let them themselves look blind,
　　Watch, gaze, and mark, till they to madness run;

While you, mine eyes, enjoy full sight of love,
Contented that such happinesses move.

---

1. Cf. Wyatt's 'Take heed betime lest ye be spied. / Your loving eyes ye cannot hide …'.

False hope, which feeds but to destroy, and spill
    What it first breeds; unnatural to the birth
    Of thine own womb, conceiving but to kill,
    And plenty gives to make the greater dearth.[1]

So tyrants do who, falsely ruling earth,   5
    Outwardly grace them, and with profit's fill
    Advance those who appointed are to death,
    To make their greater fall to please their will.

Thus shadow[2] they their wicked vile intent,
    Colouring evil with a show of good,   10
    While in fair shows their malice so is spent:
    Hope kills the heart, and tyrants shed the blood.

For hope deluding brings us to the pride[3]
Of our desires, the farther down to slide.

---

1. See Daniel, *Delia*, 23: 'False hope prolongs my ever certain grief ...'.
2. shadow] Conceal.
3. pride] Peak of success or of sexual excitement.

How well, poor heart, thou witness canst I love,
    How oft my grief hath made thee shed forth tears,
    Drops of thy dearest blood, and how oft fears
    Borne, testimony of the pains I prove;

What torments hast thou suffered, while above   5
    Joy thou tortured wert with racks which longing bears;
    Pinched with desires which yet but wishing rears,
    Firm in my faith, in constancy to move.[1]

Yet is it said, that sure love cannot be
    Where so small show of passion is descried,   10
    When thy chief pain is, that I must it hide
    From all save only one, who should it see.

For know, more passion in my heart doth move,
Than in a million that make show of love.[2]

---

1. Suffering from desires that wishing, firm in my faithful love, still wishes to
   rear, to move in constancy.
2. See *AS* 54. 13–14: 'Dumb swans, not chatt'ring 'pies do Lovers prove; / They
   love indeed who quake to say they love.

You happy blessèd eyes,
 Which in that ruling place
 Have force both to delight, and to disgrace,
Whose light allures and ties
 All hearts to your command: 5
 O, look on me, who do at mercy stand.

'Tis you that rule my life,
 'Tis you my comforts give,
 Then let not scorn to me my ending drive;
Nor let the frowns of strife   10
 Have might to hurt those lights
 Which while they shine they are true love's delights.

See but when night appears,
 And sun has lost his force,
 How his loss doth all joy from us divorce; 15
And when he shines, and clears
 The heav'ns from clouds of night,
 How happy then is made our gazing sight.

But more than sun's fair light
 Your beams do seem to me,   20
 Whose sweetest looks do tie and yet make free;
Why should you then so spite
 Poor me, as to destroy
 The only pleasure that I taste of joy?

Shine then, O dearest lights,   25
 With favour and with love,
 And let no cause your cause of frownings move;
But as the soul's delights
 So bless my then-blest eyes,
 Which unto you their true affection ties. 30

Then shall the sun give place
    As to your greater might,
    Yielding that you do show more perfect light.
O then but grant this grace
    Unto your love-tied slave,   35
    To shine on me, who to you all faith gave.

And when you please to frown,
    Use your most killing eyes
    On them who in untruth and falsehood lies,
But, dear, on me cast down   40
    Sweet looks, for true desire,
    That banish do all thoughts of feignèd fire.

Night, welcome art thou to my mind distressed,
    Dark, heavy, sad, yet not more sad than I:
    Never could'st thou find fitter company
    For thine own humour than I, thus oppressed.

If thou beest dark, my wrongs still unredressed   5
    Saw never light, nor smallest bliss can spy;
    If heavy, joy from me too fast doth hie,
    And care outgoes my hope of quiet rest.

Then now in friendship join with hapless me,
    Who am as sad and dark as thou canst be,   10
    Hating all pleasure or delight of life;

Silence, and grief, with thee I best do love,
    And from you three I know I cannot move:
    Then let us live companions without strife.[1]

---

1.   See *AS* 96, for the union of Night, Silence and Grief.

What pleasure can a banished creature have
    In all the pastimes that invented are
    By wit or learning, absence making war
    Against all peace that may a biding[1] crave?

 Can we delight but in a welcome grave   5
    Where we may bury pains, and so be far
    From loathèd company, who always jar
    Upon the string of mirth that pastime gave?

The knowing part of joy is deemed the heart;
    If that be gone, what joy can joy impart,   10
    When senseless is the feeler of our mirth?

No, I am banished, and no good shall find,
    But all my fortunes must with mischief bind,
    Who but for misery did gain a birth.

---

1. biding] Continuance or residence.

If I were giv'n to mirth, 'twould be more cross
　Thus to be robbèd of my chiefest joy,
　But silently I bear my greatest loss;
　Who's used to sorrow, grief will not destroy.

Nor can I, as those pleasant wits,[1] enjoy　　　　　　5
　My own framed words, which I account the dross
　Of purer thoughts, or reckon them as moss,
　While they, wit-sick, themselves to breathe employ.

Alas, think I, your plenty shows your want,
　For where most feeling is, words are more scant.　　10
　Yet pardon me, live, and your pleasure take;

Grudge not if I, neglected, envy show;[2]
　'Tis not to you that I dislike do owe,
　But, crossed myself, wish some like me to make.

---

1. The contrast between other 'wits' and the writer's inadequacies is a common theme in AS; e.g. 3 and 50.
2. See RS 1. 3: 'Grudge not if I …'.

It is not love which you poor fools do deem,
   That doth appear by fond and outward shows
   Of kissing, toying, or by swearing's gloze: [1]
   O no, these are far off from Love's esteem.

Alas, they are not such that can redeem   5
   Love lost, or winning, keep those chosen blows;
   Though oft with face and looks Love overthrows,
   Yet so slight conquest doth not him beseem.

'Tis not a show of sighs or tears can prove
   Who loves indeed, which blasts of feignèd love   10
   Increase or die, as favours from them slide;

But in the soul true love in safety lies,
   Guarded by faith, which to desert still hies;
   And yet kind looks do many blessings hide.

---

1.   swearing's gloze] Deceptive flattering oaths.

You blessèd stars which do Heav'ns glory show,[1]
   And at your brightness make our eyes admire:
   Yet envy not, though I on earth below
   Enjoy a sight which moves in me more fire.

I do confess such beauty breeds desire,   5
   You shine, and clearest light on us bestow,
   Yet doth a sight on earth more warmth inspire
   Into my loving soul, his grace to know.

Clear, bright and shining as you are, is this
   Light of my joy,[2] fixed steadfast, nor will move   10
   His light from me, nor I change from his love,
   But still increase, as th'height of all my bliss.

His sight gives life unto my love-ruled eyes,
My love content, because in his, love lies.

---

1.   See *RS* 1: 'You purest stars, whose never dying fires / Deck heavenly spheres, and rule the world below, / Grudge not if I in your clear beauties know / The fair maid's eyes, the stars of my desires. / To earthly hearts your light, which not expires, / Makes known the matchless place wherein you go, / And they the mind which through them shines do show, / Whose clearest beams, my soul as heaven admires: / You shine still one, and alter not your race / At suit of those which most your lights adore, / For well you know, you shine for heaven's grace. / And they in whom all eyes on earth are blessed, / Though than the heavenly lights I love them more, / Shine to the world, and me but with the rest.'

2.   See also *AS* 68: 'Light of my life … paradise of joy …'.

If ever love had force in human breast,
   If ever he could move in pensive heart,
   Or if that he such pow'r could but impart
   To breed those flames whose heat brings joy's unrest,

Then look on me: I am to these addressed,[1]   5
   I[2] am the soul that feels the greatest smart,
   I am that heartless trunk of heart's depart,
   And I that one by love and grief oppressed.

None ever felt the truth of love's great miss
   Of eyes, till I deprivèd was of bliss;   10
   For had he seen, he must have pity showed;

I should not have been made this stage[3] of woe,
   Where sad disasters have their open show:
   O no, more pity he had sure bestowed.

---

1.   addressed] Assigned, given over to.
2.   MS has commas after 'I' here and in the next two lines, perhaps for emphasis.
3.   stage] A stage in a theatre, or a punishment scaffold.

Sorrow, I yield, and grieve that I did miss:
Will not thy rage be satisfied with this?
   As sad a devil as thee,
   Made me unhappy be;
Wilt thou not yet consent to leave, but still   5
Strive how to show thy cursèd, devil'sh skill?

I mourn, and dying am; what would you more?
My soul attends, to leave this cursèd shore
   Where harms do only flow,
   Which teach me but to know   10
The saddest hours[1] of my life's unrest,
And tired minutes with grief's hand oppressed.

Yet all this will not pacify thy spite:
No, nothing can bring ease but my last night.
   Then quickly let it be,   15
   While I unhappy see
That Time, so sparing to grant lovers bliss,
Will see, for time lost, there shall no grief miss.

Nor let me ever cease from lasting grief,
But endless let it be, without relief,   20
   To win again of Love
   The favour I did prove,
And with my end please him, since, dying, I
Have him offended, yet unwillingly.

---

1. hours] Disyllabic.

O dearest eyes, the lights and guides of love,
   The joys of Cupid who, himself born blind,
   To your bright shining doth his triumphs bind,
   For in your seeing doth his glory move.

How happy are those places where you prove   5
   Your heav'nly beams, which makes the sun to find
   Envy and grudging, he so long hath shined,
   For your clear lights to match his beams above.

But now, alas, your sight is here forbid,
   And darkness must these poor lost rooms possess,   10
   So be all blessèd lights from henceforth hid,
   That this black deed of darkness have excess.

For why should heaven afford least light to those
Who for my misery such darkness chose?

44.

How fast thou hast'st, O Spring, with sweetest speed
   To catch thy waters which before are run,
   And of the greater rivers welcome won,
   Ere these thy newborn streams these places feed.

Yet you do well, lest staying here might breed   5
   Dangerous floods,[1] your sweetest banks t'o'er-run,
   And yet much better my distress to shun,
   Which makes my tears your swiftest course succeed;

But best you do when with so hasty flight
   You fly my ills, which now my self outgo,   10
   Whose broken heart can testify such woe
   That, so o'ercharged, my life blood wasteth quite.

Sweet Spring, then keep your way, be never spent,
And my ill days, or griefs, asunder rent.

---

1. floods] Her tears might cause the streams to overflow; cf. Donne's 'The
    Canonisation', 13: 'Who says my tears have overflowed his ground?'

Good now, be still,[1] and do not me torment
 With multitudes of questions, be at rest,
 And only let me quarrel with my breast,
 Which still lets in new storms my soul to rent.

Fie, will you still my mischiefs more augment?   5
 You say I answer cross,[2] I that confessed
 Long since; yet must I ever be oppressed
 With your tongue-torture which will ne'er be spent?

Well then, I see no way but this will fright
 That devil speech: alas, I am possessed,   10
 And mad folks senseless are of wisdom's right;

The hellish spirit, Absence, doth arrest
 All my poor senses to his cruel might:
 Spare me then till I am my self, and blest.

---

1.   For the lover's response to a friend's well-meant criticism, see also *AS* 14 and
   21, and Donne's 'The Canonisation'.
2.   cross] In contrary or perverse fashion.

Love, thou hast all, for now thou hast me made
    So thine, as if for thee I were ordained;
    Then take thy conquest, nor let me be pained
    More in thy sun, when I do seek thy shade.

No place for help have I left to invade,   5
    That showed a face where least ease might be gained;
    Yet found I pain increase, and but obtained[1]
    That this no way was to have love allayed,

When hot and thirsty, to a well I came,
    Trusting by that to quench part of my flame,   10
    But there I was by love afresh embraced;

Drink I could not, but in it I did see
    Myself a living glass as well as she,
    For Love to see himself in, truly placed.

---

1.   but obtained] And merely discovered that ...

O stay, mine eyes, shed not these fruitless tears,
    Since hope is past to win you back again
    That treasure which, being lost, breeds all your pain;
    Cease from this poor betraying of your fears.

Think this too childish is, for where grief rears   5
    So high a pow'r for such a wretched gain,
    Sighs nor laments should thus be spent in vain:
    True sorrow never outward wailing bears.

Be ruled by me, keep all the rest in store,
    Till no room is that may contain one more,   10
    Then in that sea of tears drown hapless me,

And I'll provide such store of sighs, as part
    Shall be enough to break the strongest heart;
    This done, we shall from torments freèd be.

How like a fire doth love increase in me,
   The longer that it lasts, the stronger still,
   The greater, purer, brighter, and doth fill
   No eye with wonder more; then hopes still be

Bred in my breast, when fires of love are free   5
   To use that part to their best pleasing will,[1]
   And now impossible it is to kill
   The heat so great, where Love his strength doth see.

Mine eyes can scarce sustain the flames, my heart
   Doth trust in them my passions to impart,   10
   And languishingly strive to show my love;

My breath not able is to breathe least part
   Of that increasing fuel of my smart;
   Yet love I will, till I but ashes prove.[2]
                    Pamphilia.

---

1.   will] Possible play on 'Will', for William Herbert (also in l. 14).
2.   See *RS* 12. 12–14: 'I yield, I love, to you, than erst, I burn / More hot, more pure, like wood oft warm before, / But to you burnt to dust, can burn no more'. The signature, 'Pamphilia', marks the end of the first section.

Sonnet.

    Let grief as far be from your dearest breast
        As I do wish, or in my hands to ease;
        Then should it banished be, and sweetest rest
        Be placed to give content by love to please.

    Let those disdains which on your heart do seize   5
        Doubly return to bring her soul's unrest,
        Since true love will not that belov'd displease,
        Or let least smart to their minds be addressed;

    But oftentimes mistakings be in love.
        Be they as far from false accusing right,   10
        And still truth govern with a constant might,
        So shall you only wishèd pleasures prove.

    And as for me, she that shows you least scorn,
    With all despite and hate, be her heart torn.

Song.

O me, the time is come to part,
    And with it my life-killing smart:
Fond hope leave me, my dear must go
    To meet more joy, and I more woe.

Where still of mirth enjoy thy fill,   5
    One is enough to suffer ill:
My heart so well to sorrow used
    Can better be by new griefs bruised.

Thou whom the Heav'ns themselves like made
    Should never sit in mourning shade: 10
No, I alone must mourn and end,
    Who have a life in grief to spend.

My swiftest pace, to wailings bent,
    Shows joy had but a short time lent
To bide in me, where woes must dwell,   15
    And charm me with their cruel spell.

And yet when they their witchcrafts try,
    They only make me wish to die:
But ere my faith in love they change,
    In horrid darkness will I range.   20

Say Venus how long have I loved, and served you here,
    Yet all my passions scorned or doubted, although clear?
Alas, think love deserveth love, and you have loved:
    Look on my pains, and see if you the like have proved.
Remember then you are the Goddess of Desire,   5
    And that your sacred pow'r hath touched and felt this fire.

Persuade these flames in me to cease, or them redress
    In me, poor me, who storms of love have in excess.
My restless nights may show for me, how much I love,
    My sighs unfeigned can witness what my heart doth prove,   10
My saddest looks do show the grief my soul endures,
    Yet all these torments from your hands no help procures.

Command that wayward child your son to grant your right,[1]
    And that his bow and shafts he yield to your fair sight,
To you who have the eyes of joy, the heart of love,   15
    And then new hopes may spring, that I may pity move:
Let him not triumph that he can both hurt and save,
    And more, brag that to you yourself a wound he gave.

Rule him, or what shall I expect of good to see,
Since he that hurt you, he alas may murder me?   20

---

1.   See *AS* 20. 2: 'See there that boy, that murthring boy, I say …'.

Song.

I, that am of all most crossed,
Having, and that had, have lost,
May with reason thus complain,
Since love breeds love, and love's pain.

That which I did most desire   5
To allay my loving fire,
I may have, yet now must miss,
Since another ruler is.

Would that I no ruler had,
Or the service not so bad,   10
Then might I with bliss enjoy
That which now my hopes destroy.

And that wicked pleasure got,
Brings with it the sweetest lot:
I, that must not taste the best,   15
Fed, must starve, and restless rest.

Song.

Love as well can make abiding
   In a faithful shepherd's breast
As in princes', whose thoughts sliding
   Like swift rivers never rest.

Change, to their minds, is best feeding,   5
   To a shepherd all his care,
Who, when his love is exceeding,
   Thinks his faith his richest fare;

Beauty, but a slight inviting,
   Cannot stir his heart to change;   10
Constancy, his chief delighting,
   Strives to flee from fancies strange;

Fairness to him is no pleasure,
   If in other than his love;
Nor can esteem that a treasure   15
   Which in her smiles doth not move.

This a shepherd once confessed,
   Who loved well but was not loved;
Though with scorn and grief oppressed,
   Could not yet to change be moved.   20

But himself he thus contented,
   While in love he was accursed:
This hard hap he not repented,
   Since best lovers speed the worst.

Song.

Dearest, if I, by my deserving,
  May maintain in your thoughts my love,
    Let me it still enjoy,
    Nor faith destroy,
But pity love where it doth move.   5

Let no other new love invite you
  To leave me who so long have served,
    Nor let your pow'r decline,
    But purely shine
On me, who have all truth preserved;   10

Or had you once found my heart straying,
  Then would I not accuse your change,
    But being constant still,
    It needs must kill
One whose soul knows not how to range.   15

Yet may you love's sweet smiles recover,
  Since all love is not yet quite lost,
    But tempt not love too long,
    Lest so great wrong
Make him think he is too much crossed.   20

Song.

Fairest and still truest eyes,
Can you the lights be, and the spies
    Of my desires?
Can you shine clear for love's delight,
And yet the breeders be of spite,   5
    And jealous fires?[1]

Mark what looks you do behold,
Such as by jealousy are told
    They want your love;
See how they sparkle in distrust,   10
Which by a heat of thoughts unjust
    In them do move.

Learn to guide your course by art,
Change your eyes into your heart,
    And patient be,   15
Till fruitless jealousy gives leave
By safest absence to receive
    What you would see;

Then let Love his triumph have,
And suspicion such a grave   20
    As not to move,
While wishèd freedom brings that bliss,
That you enjoy what all joy is,
    Happy to love.

---

1. The beloved is urged to observe how others, provoked by his charms and
driven by ungenerous feelings, seek his love without feeling true love for him,
and to wait until they give up, so as to be able to experience the true joy of
confident love (with her). See P39.

       Sonnet. 1.

In night yet may we see some kind of light,
    When as the moon doth please to show her face
    And in the sun's room yields her light and grace,
    Which otherwise must suffer dullest night.

So are my fortunes, barred from true delight,   5
    Cold and uncertain, like to this strange place,
    Decreasing, changing in an instant space,
    And even at full of joy turned to despite.

Justly on Fortune was bestowed the wheel,
    Whose favours fickle and unconstant reel,   10
    Drunk with delight of change and sudden pain;

Where pleasure hath no settled place of stay,
    But turning still, for our best hopes decay,
    And this, alas, we lovers often gain.

2.

Love like a juggler comes to play his prize,
   And all minds draw his wonders to admire,
   To see how cunningly he, wanting eyes,
   Can yet deceive the best sight of desire.

The wanton child, how he can feign his fire   5
   So prettily, as none sees his disguise,
   How finely do his tricks, while we fools hire
   The badge and office of his tyrannies!

For in the end, such juggling he doth make,
   As he our hearts instead of eyes doth take;   10
   For men can only by their sleights abuse

The sight with nimble and delightful skill;
   But if he play, his gain is our lost will;
   Yet childlike, we cannot his sports refuse.

Most blessèd night, the happy time for love,
    The shade for lovers, and their love's delight,
    The reign of love for servants free from spite,
    The hopeful season for joy's sports to move:

Now hast thou made thy glory higher prove   5
    Than did the god whose pleasant reed did smite
    All Argus' eyes into a deathlike night,
    Till they were safe, that none could love reprove;[1]

Now thou hast closed those eyes from prying sight,
    That nourish jealousy more than joys right,   10
    While vain suspicion fosters their mistrust,

Making sweet sleep to master all suspect,
    Which else their private fears would not neglect,
    But would embrace both blinded, and unjust.

---

1. Mercury, playing on Syrinx's pipe, lulled thousand-eyed Argus to sleep, and killed him (Ovid, *Metamorphoses* I); Stella also fears watchful Argus eyes: *AS* 11.

4.

Cruel suspicion, O! be now at rest,
    Let daily torments bring to thee some stay;
    Alas, make not my ill thy easeful prey,
    Nor give loose reins to rage, when love's oppressed.

I am by care sufficiently distressed;   5
    No rack can stretch my heart more, nor a way
    Can I find out for least content to lay
    One happy foot of joy, one step that's blest.

But to my end thou fliest with greedy eye,
    Seeking to bring grief by base jealousy;   10
    O, in how strange a cage am I kept in!

No little sign of favour can I prove
    But must be weighed, and turned to wronging love,
    And with each humour must my state begin.

How many nights have I with pain endured,
    Which as so many ages I esteemed,
    Since my misfortune, yet no whit redeemed
    But rather faster tied, to grief assured?

How many hours have my sad thoughts endured   5
    Of killing pains? Yet is it not esteemed
    By cruel Love, who might have these redeemed,
    And all these years of hours to joy assured:

But, fond child, had he had a care to save
    As first to conquer, this my pleasure's grave   10
    Had not been now to testify my woe;

I might have been an image of delight,
    As now a tomb for sad misfortune's spite,
    Which Love unkindly for reward doth show.

My pain, still smothered in my grievèd breast,
    Seeks for some ease, yet cannot passage find
    To be discharged of this unwelcome guest;
    When most I strive, more fast his burdens bind.

Like to a ship on Goodwins[1] cast by wind,   5
    The more she strives, more deep in sand is pressed,
    Till she be lost, so am I, in this kind,
    Sunk, and devoured, and swallowed by unrest,

Lost, shipwrecked, spoiled, debarred of smallest hope,[2]
    Nothing of pleasure left; save thoughts have scope,   10
    Which wander may. Go then, my thoughts, and cry

Hope's perished, Love tempest-beaten, Joy lost.
    Killing Despair hath all these blessings crossed,[3]
    Yet Faith still cries, Love will not falsify.

---

1.   Goodwins] The Goodwin Sands, off the Kentish coast, where many ships
     were wrecked.
2.   The common analogy of the lover and imperilled ship derives ultimately
     from Petrarch, *Rime* 189.
3.   crossed] Thwarted.

An end, fond jealousy: alas, I know
    Thy hiddenest and thy most secret art;
    Thou canst no new invention frame, but part
    I have already seen, and felt with woe.

All thy dissemblings which by feignèd show   5
    Won my belief, while truth did rule my heart,
    I with glad mind embraced, and deemed my smart
    The spring of joy, whose streams with bliss should flow.

I thought excuses had been reasons true,
    And that no falsehood could of thee ensue,   10
    So soon belief in honest minds is wrought;

But now I find thy flattery and skill,
    Which idly made me to observe thy will:
    Thus is my learning by my bondage bought.

Poor Love in chains and fetters, like a thief,
    I met led forth, as chaste Diana's gain,
    Vowing the untaught lad should no relief
    From her receive, who gloried in fond pain.[1]

She called him thief; with vows he did maintain   5
    He never stole, but some sad slight[2] of grief
    Had giv'n to those who did his pow'r disdain,
    In which revenge, his honour, was the chief.

She said he murdered, and therefore must die;
    He, that he caused but love, did harms deny.   10
    But while she thus discoursing with him stood,

The nymphs untied him, and his chains took off,
    Thinking him safe; but he, loose, made a scoff,
    Smiling, and scorning them, flew to the wood.

---

1.   For Cupid punished and escaping, see *AS* 17, and Fulke Greville, *Caelica* 13.
2.   slight] Small amount.

Pray do not use these words, 'I must be gone'.
   Alas, do not foretell mine ills to come,
   Let not my care be to my joys a tomb,
   But rather find my loss with loss alone.

Cause me not thus a more distressèd one,   5
   Not feeling bliss because of this sad doom
   Of present cross, for thinking will o'ercome
   And lose all pleasure, since grief breedeth none.

Let the misfortune come at once to me,
   Nor suffer me with grief to punished be;   10
   Let me be ignorant of mine own ill,

Than with the fore-knowledge quite to lose
   That which, with so much care and pains, love chose
   For his reward: but joy now, then mirth kill.

Folly would needs make me a lover be,
  When I did little think of loving thought,
  Or ever to be tied, while she told me
  That none can live but to these bands are brought.[1]

I, ignorant, did grant, and so was bought,   5
  And sold again to lovers' slavery;
  The duty to that vanity once taught,[2]
  Such band is, as we will not seek to free.

Yet when I well did understand his might,
  How he[3] inflamed, and forced one[4] to affect,   10
  I loved and smarted, counting it delight
  So still to waste, which Reason did reject.

When Love came blindfold, and did challenge[5] me:
Indeed I loved, but, wanton boy, not he.

---

1. Paulissen prints (p. 139) an early MS version: l.1: 'Cupid would …'; l.3: 'hee …'; l. 4: 'his bands …'.
2. Paulissen: 'to the god of love once …'.
3. he] Cupid, the 'wanton boy'.
4. Paulissen: 'forced me …'.
5. challenge] Lay claim to.

Song.

The spring time of my first loving
   Finds yet no winter of removing,
Nor frosts to make my hopes decrease,
   But with the summer still increase.[1]

The trees may teach us love's remaining,   5
   Who suffer change with little paining:
Though winter make their leaves decrease,
   Yet with the summer they increase.

As birds by silence show their mourning
   In cold, yet sing at spring's returning,   10
So may love, nipped awhile, decrease,
   But as the summer soon increase.

Those that do love but for a season,
   Do falsify both love and reason,
For reason wills, if love decrease,   15
   It like the summer should increase.

Though love some times may be mistaken,
   The truth yet ought not to be shaken,
Or though the heat awhile decrease,
   It with the summer may increase.   20

And since the spring time of my loving
   Found never winter of removing,
Nor frosts to make my hopes decrease,
   Shall as the summer still increase.

---

1. See also Donne's 'Love's Growth'.

Song.

Love, a child, is ever crying,
Please him, and he straight is flying,
Give him, he the more is craving,
Never satisfied with having.

His desires have no measure,   5
Endless folly is his treasure,
What he promiseth he breaketh,
Trust not one word that he speaketh.

He vows nothing but false matter,
And to cozen you he'll flatter,   10
Let him gain the hand, he'll leave you,
And still glory to deceive you.

He will triumph in your wailing,
And yet cause be of your failing:
These his virtues are, and slighter   15
Are his gifts, his favours lighter.

Feathers are as firm in staying,
Wolves no fiercer in their preying.
As a child then leave him crying,
Nor seek him, so giv'n to flying.   20

Being past the pains of love,
Freedom gladly seeks to move,
Says that love's delights were pretty,
But to dwell in them 'twere pity;

And yet truly says that love　　　　　　　5
Must of force in all hearts move,
But though his delights are pretty,
To dwell in them were a pity.

Let love slightly pass like love,
Never let it too deep move,　　　　　　　10
For though love's delights are pretty,
To dwell in them were great pity.

Love no pity hath of love,
Rather griefs than pleasures move,
So though his delights are pretty,　　　　15
To dwell in them would be pity.

Those that like the smart of love,
In them let it freely move,
Else, though his delights are pretty,
Do not dwell in them, for pity.　　　　　20

[P76]   O pardon, Cupid, I confess my fault:
              Then mercy grant me in so just a kind,
              For treason never lodgèd in my mind
              Against thy might, so much as in a thought.

         And now my folly have I dearly bought,   5
              Nor could my soul least rest or quiet find
              Since rashness did my thoughts to error bind,
              Which now thy fury, and my harm, hath wrought.

         I curse that thought and hand which that first framed
              For which by thee I am most justly blamed;   10
              But now that hand shall guided be aright,

         And give a crown unto thy endless praise,
              Which shall thy glory, and thy greatness raise
              More than these poor things could thy honour spite.

A Crown of Sonnets Dedicated
to LOVE

[P77]   In this strange labyrinth[1] how shall I turn?
       Ways are on all sides, while the way I miss:
       If to the right hand, there in love I burn;
       Let me go forward, therein danger is.

     If to the left,[2] suspicion hinders bliss;   5
       Let me turn back, shame cries I ought return,
       Nor faint, though crosses[3] with my fortune kiss;
       Stand still is harder, although sure to mourn.

     Thus let me take the right, or left hand way,
       Go forward, or stand still, or back retire: 10
       I must these doubts endure without allay
       Or help, but travail[4] find for my best hire.

     Yet that which most my troubled sense doth move,
     Is to leave all, and take the thread of Love.

---

1.   labyrinth] Petrarch, Sonnet CCII: 'I have entered the labyrinth from which
     I see no escape'; the myth of Ariadne's rescue of Theseus from the Minotaur
     was used by various Renaissance sonneteers.
2.   The right hand was associated with good fortune, the left with bad, the sin-
     ister; to go 'forward' might be too 'forward', or bold.
3.   crosses] Confusing intersections in the maze, or troubles.
4.   travail] Texts read both 'travail' and 'travel'; the pun was a common one.

Is to leave all, and take the thread of Love,
  Which line straight leads unto the soul's content,
  Where choice delights with pleasure's wings do move,
  And idle fancy never room had lent.[1]

When chaste thoughts guide us, then our minds are bent   5
  To take that good which ills from us remove:
  Light of true love brings fruit which none repent,
  But constant lovers seek, and wish to prove.

Love is the shining star of blessing's light,
  The fervent fire of zeal, the root of peace,   10
  The lasting lamp, fed with the oil of right,
  Image of faith, and womb for joy's increase.

Love is true virtue, and his ends delight;
His flames are joys, his bands true lovers' might.

---

1. See Spenser's *Amoretti* 76, for 'vertue', 'delight', 'wanton wings', 'fruit', cata-
    logue, 'nest of love' and 'bowre of blisse'.

His flames are joys, his bands true lovers' might,
   No stain is there, but pure, as purest white,
   Where no cloud[1] can appear to dim his light,[2]
   Nor spot defile, but shame will soon requite.

Here are affections tried by Love's just might,[3]   5
   As gold by fire,[4] and black discerned by white,
   Error by truth, and darkness known by light,
   Where faith is valued for Love to requite.

Please him, and serve him, glory in his might,
   And firm he'll be, as innocency white,   10
   Clear as th'air, warm as sun's beams, as day light,
   Just as truth, constant as fate, joyed to requite.

Then Love obey, strive to observe his might,
And be in his brave Court a glorious light.

---

1.   cloud] In *OA* 42, the would-be adulteress Gynecia pleads for 'cloudie feares' to close her eyes.
2.   See Sidney's monorhymed sonnet, *Arcadia,* Book Three (*OA* 42): 'How is my sun, whose beams are shining bright …', which uses the same rhymes, 'might' and 'light'.
3.   See Spenser, *Amoretti* 84, for 'spotlesse', 'affections' and final injunction.
4.   fire] The refining power of love was frequently compared to the effect on gold of fire (see Cardinal Bembo in Castiglione, *The Book of the Courtier*).

4.

And be in his brave Court a glorious light:
    Shine in the eyes of faith and constancy,
    Maintain the fires of love still burning bright,
    Not slightly sparkling, but light flaming be,

Never to slack till earth no stars can see,   5
    Till sun and moon do leave us to dark night,
    And second chaos[1] once again do free
    Us and the world from all division's spite.

Till then, affections, which his followers are,
    Govern our hearts, and prove his power's gain   10
    To taste this pleasing sting, seek with all care,
    For happy smarting is it, with small pain;

Such as, although it pierce your tender heart
And burn, yet burning you will love the smart.

---

1. chaos] At the end of the world, in Neoplatonic thought, matter would revert
   to primeval chaos.

And burn, yet burning you will love the smart,
    When you shall feel the weight of true desire,
    So pleasing, as you would not wish your part
    Of burden should be missing from that fire;

But faithful and unfeignèd heat aspire,   5
    Which sin abolisheth, and doth impart[1]
    Salves to all fear, with virtues which inspire
    Souls with divine love, which shows his chaste art,

And guide he[2] is to joyings; open eyes
    He hath to happiness, and best can learn   10
    Us means how to deserve: this he descries,
    Who, blind, yet doth our hiddenest thoughts discern.

Thus we may gain, since living in blest love,
He may our prophet[3] and our tutor prove.

---

1. impart] The faithful and unfeigned heat of true love abolishes sin and imparts cures for all wrong fears.
2. he] Love, Cupid.
3. prophet] There is a pun on 'profit' (in MS).

He may our prophet and our tutor prove,[1]
   In whom alone we do this power find,
   To join two hearts as in one frame to move,
   Two bodies, but one soul to move the mind,

Eyes, which must care to one dear object bind,   5
   Ears to each other's speech, as if above
   All else they sweet and learnèd were; this kind
   Content of lovers witnesseth true love:

It doth enrich the wits, and make you see
   That in yourself which you knew not before,   10
   Forcing you to admire such gifts should be
   Hid from your knowledge, yet in you the store.

Millions of these adorn the throne of Love,
How blest be they then, who his favours prove.[2]

---

1. prove] Turn out to be.
2. prove] Experience.

How blest be they then, who his favours prove,
    A life whereof the birth is just desire,
    Breeding sweet flame, which hearts invite to move
    In these loved eyes which kindle Cupid's fire,

And nurse his longings with his thoughts entire,   5
    Fixed on the heat of wishes formed by love;
    Yet whereas fire destroys, this doth aspire,
    Increase, and foster all delights above.

Love will a painter[1] make you, such, as you
    Shall able be to draw your only dear   10
    More lively, perfect, lasting and more true[2]
    Than rarest workman, and to you more near.

These be the least, then all must needs confess,
He that shuns love doth love himself the less.

---

1.   painter] Cf. *AS* 38. 6–7: 'Stella's image, wrought / By Love's own self …'.
2.   more true] A more accurate likeness; also, a more faithful lover.

He that shuns love doth love himself the less,
   And cursèd he whose spirit not admires
   The worth[1] of love, where endless blessedness
   Reigns, and commands, maintained by heav'nly fires

Made of virtue, joined by truth, blown by desires,   5
   Strengthened by worth, renewed by carefulness,
   Flaming in never-changing thoughts: briars
   Of jealousy shall here miss welcomeness,

Nor coldly pass in the pursuits of love,
   Like one long frozen in a sea of ice;   10
   And yet but chastely let your passions move,
   Nor thought from virtuous love your minds entice.

Never to other ends your fancies place,
But where they may return with honour's grace.

---

1. worth] Possibly (as elsewhere) a play on 'Wroth'.

But where they may return with honour's grace,
  Where Venus' follies can no harbour win,
  But chasèd are, as worthless of the face
  Or style of Love, who hath lascivious been.

Our hearts are subject to her son, where sin   5
  Never did dwell, or rest one minute's space;
  What faults he hath, in her did still begin,
  And from her breast he sucked his fleeting pace.

If lust be counted love, 'tis falsely named
  By wickedness, a fairer gloss to set   10
  Upon that vice which else makes men ashamed
  In the own[1] phrase to warrant,[2] but beget

This child for love, who ought, like monster born,
Be from the Court of Love and reason torn.

---

1. the own] Their own.
2. warrant] Acknowledge, admit to.

Be from the Court of Love and Reason torn,
    For Love in Reason now doth put his trust,
    Desert and liking are together born
    Children of Love and Reason, parents just.

Reason adviser is, Love ruler must   5
    Be of the State, which crown he long hath worn,
    Yet so, as neither will in least mistrust
    The government where no fear is born of scorn.

Then reverence both their mights thus made of one,
    But wantonness and all those errors shun,   10
    Which wrongers be, impostures, and alone
    Maintainers of all follies ill begun:[1]

Fruit of a sour, and unwholesome ground,
Unprofitably pleasing, and unsound.

---

1.   The rhyme scheme of these four lines is *cdcd*.

Unprofitably pleasing, and unsound,
    When Heaven[1] gave liberty to frail dull earth
    To bring forth plenty that in ills abound,
    Which ripest yet do bring a certain dearth.

A timeless and unseasonable birth,   5
    Planted in ill, in worse time springing found,
    Which hemlock-like[2] might feed a sick-wit's[3] mirth,
    Where unruled vapours[4] swim in endless round.

Then joy we not in what we ought to shun,
    Where shady pleasures show, but true-born fires   10
    Are quite quenched out, or by poor ashes won
    Awhile to keep those cool and wan desires.

O no, let Love his glory have, and might
Be given to him, who triumphs in his right.

---

1. Heaven] See Genesis 50: xi.
2. See *RS* 64: 'But, alas, why do you nourish / Poisonous weeds of cold despair / In love's garden …'.
3. sick-wit] One psychologically disturbed, or perversely witty.
4. vapours] Exhalations thought to be produced within the body, causing psychological disorders.

Be given to him, who triumphs in his right,
 Nor fading be, but like those blossoms fair
 Which fall for good, and lose their colours bright,
 Yet die not, but with fruit their loss repair.

So may love make you pale with loving care,   5
 When sweet enjoying shall restore that light
 More clear in beauty than we can compare,
 If not to Venus in her chosen night.

And who so give themselves in this dear kind,
 These happinesses shall attend them, still   10
 To be supplied with joys, enriched in mind,
 With treasures of content, and pleasure's fill.

Thus Love to be divine doth here appear,
Free from all fogs, but shining fair and clear.

Free from all fogs, but shining fair and clear,
    Wise in all good, and innocent in ill,
    Where holy friendship is esteemèd dear,
    With truth in love, and justice in our will.

In Love these titles only have their fill   5
    Of happy life-maintainer, and the mere
    Defence [1] of right, the punisher of skill
    And fraud; from whence directions doth appear.

To thee then, Lord commander of all hearts,
    Ruler of our affections, kind and just,   10
    Great King of Love, my soul from feignèd smarts [2]
    Or thought of change I offer to your trust

This crown, my self, and all that I have more,
Except my heart, which you bestowed before.

---

1.   mere / Defence] Absolute, perfect defender.
2.   feignèd smarts] MS reads 'fained', making the precise intention unclear:
     either 'fained smarts', sufferings endured perforce, or 'feigned smarts', insin-
     cere mistreatments; the loose sentence structure does not help.

Except my heart, which you bestowed before,
    And for a sign of conquest gave away
    As worthless to be kept in your choice store,
    Yet one more spotless with you doth not stay.

The tribute which my heart doth truly pay   5
    Is faith untouched, pure thoughts discharge the score[1]
    Of debts for me, where Constancy bears sway,
    And rules as Lord, unharmed by envy's sore.

Yet other mischiefs fail not to attend,
    As enemies to you, my foes must be:[2]   10
    Curst jealousy doth all her forces bend
    To my undoing; thus my harms I see.

So though in love I fervently do burn,
In this strange labyrinth how shall I turn?[3]

---

1. discharge the score] Pay.
2. Other mischiefs, attending upon me or in the Court of Love, must, as enemies to you, be my foes.
3. The last line repeats the first of the corona (P77. 1), as is correct, completing the crown (as in Donne's 'La Corona') but enclosing the labyrinth.

Sweet, let me enjoy thy sight
    More clear, more bright than morning sun,
Which in spring-time gives delight
    And by which summer's pride is won.
Present sight doth pleasures move,   5
    Which in sad absence we must miss,
But when met again in love,
    Then twice redoubled is our bliss.

Yet this comfort absence gives,
    And only faithful loving tries,   10
That, though parted, love's force lives
    As just in heart as in our eyes.
But such comfort banish quite,
    Far sweeter is it, still to find
Favour in thy lovèd sight,   15
    Which present smiles with joys combined.

Eyes of gladness, lips of love,
    And hearts from passions not to turn,
But in sweet affections move
    In flames of faith to live, and burn.   20
Dearest, then this kindness give,
    And grant me life, which is your sight,
Wherein I more blessèd live,
    Than gracèd with the sun's fair light.

Sweet Silvia in a shady wood,
    With her fair nymphs laid down,
Saw not far off where Cupid stood,
    The monarch of Love's crown,
All naked, playing with his wings,   5
    Within a myrtle[1] tree,
Which sight a sudden laughter brings,
    His godhead so to see.

And fondly they began to jest,
    With scoffing and delight,   10
Not knowing he did breed unrest,
    And that his will's his right.
When he perceiving of their scorn,
    Grew in such desp'rate rage,
Who, but for honour first was born,   15
    Could not his rage assuage,

Till shooting of his murd'ring dart,
    Which not long 'lighting[2] was,
Knowing the next way to the heart,
    Did through a poor nymph pass.   20
This shot, the others made to bow,
    Besides all those to blame,
Who scorners be, or not allow
    Of pow'rful Cupid's name.

Take heed then, nor do idly smile,   25
    Nor Love's commands despise,
For soon will he your strength beguile,
    Although he want his eyes.

---

1. myrtle] Tree sacred to Venus.
2. 'lighting] Alighting: not long in reaching its target.

3.

Come, merry Spring, delight us,
For Winter long did spite us,
In pleasure still persever,
Thy beauties ending never:
    Spring, and grow   5
    Lasting so,
With joys increasing ever.

Let cold from hence be banished,
Till hopes from me be vanished,
But bless thy dainties, growing   10
    In fullness freely flowing:
    For the Spring
All mirth is now bestowing.

Philomel[1] in this arbour   15
Makes now her loving harbour,
Yet[2] of her state complaining,
Her notes in mildness straining,
    Which, though sweet,
    Yet do meet   20
Her former luckless paining.

---

1.   Elizabethan poets frequently employed Ovid's story of the metamorphosis of
      Philomel into a nightingale after her rape by Tereus (*Metamorphoses* VI).
2.   yet] Still.

4.

Lovers, learn to speak but truth,
 Swear not, and your oaths forgo,
Give your age a constant youth,
 Vow no more than what you'll do.

Think it sacrilege to break   5
 What you promise shall in love,
And in tears what you do speak,
 Forget not, when the ends you prove.

Do not think it glory is
 To entice and then deceive,   10
Your chief honours lie in this:
 By worth[1] what won is, not to leave.

'Tis not for your fame to try
 What we, weak, not oft refuse,
In our bounty our faults lie,   15
 When you to do a fault will choose.

Fie, leave this, a greater gain
 'Tis to keep when you have won,
Than what purchased is with pain,
 Soon after in all scorn to shun.   20

For if worthless[2] to be prized,
 Why at first will you it move,
And if worthy, why despised?
 You cannot swear, and lie, and love.

Love, alas, you cannot like,   25
 'Tis but for a fashion moved,
None can choose and then dislike,
 Unless it be by falsehood proved.

---

1. worth] Possibly a play on 'Wroth'.
2. As above.

But your choice is, and your love,
    How most number to deceive,   30
As if honour's claim did move
    Like Popish law, none safe to leave.

Fly this folly, and return
    Unto truth in love, and try,
None but martyrs happy burn,   35
    More shameful ends they have that lie.

My heart is lost, what can I now expect:
　　An ev'ning fair, after a drowsy day?
　　Alas, fond fancy, this is not the way
　　To cure a mourning[2] heart, or salve neglect.

They who should help, do me and help reject,　　　　5
　　Embracing loose desires and wanton play,
　　While wanton base delights do bear the sway,
　　And impudency reigns without respect.

O Cupid, let your mother know her shame,
　　'Tis time for her to leave this youthful flame　　　10
　　Which doth dishonour her, is age's blame,
　　And takes away the greatness of thy name.

Thou God of love, she only Queen of lust,
Yet strives by weak'ning thee, to be unjust.

1.　This and the next sonnet, beginning the last sequence, with motifs of day/
　　night, Venus and Cupid, and burning hearts, may look back to P1.
2.　mourning] Thus 1621 edition; MS reads 'morning': a word-play linked with
　　line 2 may be intended.

Late in the forest I did Cupid see [1]
   Cold, wet and crying; he had lost his way,
   And, being blind, was farther like to stray,
   Which sight a kind compassion bred in me.

I kindly took and dried him, while that he,   5
   Poor child, complained he starvèd [2] was with stay,
   And pined for want of his accustomed prey,
   For none in that wild place his host would be.

I glad was of his finding, thinking sure
   This service should my freedom still procure,   10
   And in my arms I took him then unharmed,

Carrying him safe unto a myrtle bower,
   But in the way he made me feel his pow'r,
   Burning my heart, who had him kindly warmed.

---

1.   Such stories are frequent in Elizabethan sonnet sequences; see *AS* 17 and 65.
2.   starvèd] Perishing of hunger.

3.

Juno, still jealous of her husband Jove,
    Descended from above, on earth to try
    Whether she there could find his chosen love,
    Which made him from the heavens so often fly.

Close by the place where I for shade did lie   5
    She chasing came, but when she saw me move,
    'Have you not seen this way,' said she, 'to hie [1]
    One, in whom virtue never ground did prove,

'He, in whom love doth breed to stir more hate,
    Courting a wanton nymph for his delight?   10
    His name is Jupiter, my lord by fate,
    Who for her leaves me, heav'n, his throne and light.'

'I saw him not,' said I, 'although here are
Many, in whose hearts love hath made like war.'

---

1. hie] Hasten.

When I beheld the image of my dear,[1]
   With greedy looks mine eyes would that way bend,
   Fear and Desire[2] did inwardly contend,
   Fear to be marked, Desire to draw still near;

And in my soul a Spirit would appear,   5
   Which boldness warranted, and did pretend
   To be my Genius,[3] yet I durst not lend
   My eyes in trust, where others seemed so clear.

Then did I search from whence this danger 'rose,
   If such unworthiness in me did rest   10
   As my starved eyes must not with sight be blest,
   When Jealousy her poison did disclose.

Yet in my heart, unseen of jealous eye,
The truer image shall in triumph lie.

---

1. The topic of the superiority to physical reality of the lover's mental image
    (and imaginary possession) of the beloved was a common topic, e.g. Spenser,
    Amoretti 45, Donne, 'The Dream' (Elegy X).
2. Desire] 1621's capitalizations are retained here, to reflect the poem's allego-
    rized mental conflict.
3. Genius] Attendant or tutelary spirit; hence, one's true nature or character-
    istic disposition.

5.

    Like to huge clouds of smoke which well may hide
        The face of fairest day, though for a while,
        So wrong may shadow me, till truth do smile,
        And justice,[1] sun-like, hath those vapours tied.

    O doting Time, canst thou for shame let slide   5
        So many minutes, while ills do beguile
        Thy age and worth, and falsehoods thus defile
        Thy ancient good, where now but crosses bide?

    Look but once up, and leave thy toiling pace,
        And on my miseries thy dim eye place;   10
        Go not so fast, but give my care some end,

    Turn not thy glass, alas, unto my ill,
        Since thou with sand it canst not so far fill,
        But to each one my sorrows will extend.[2]

---

1. Justice] The sun was a traditional emblem of justice (*sol justitiae*).
2. Do not give me more time, which will be to my harm, as you cannot give me so much time that my sorrows will not reach every minute.

O! that no day would ever more appear,
    But cloudy night to govern this sad place,
    Nor light from heav'n these hapless rooms to grace,
    Since that light's shadowed which my love holds dear.

Let thickest mists in envy master here,   5
    And sun-born day for malice show no face,
    Disdaining light, where Cupid and the race
    Of lovers are despised, and shame shines clear.

Let me be dark, since barred of my chief light,
    And wounding Jealousy commands by might,   10
    But stage-play-like disguisèd pleasures give: [1]

To me it seems, as ancient fictions make
    The stars all fashions and all shapes partake,
    While in my thoughts true form of love shall live.

---

1. Jealousy rules, and produces pleasures that are as unreal and deceptive as plays (or masques).

No time, no room, no thought or writing can
    Give rest or quiet to my loving heart.
    Or can my memory or[1] fancy scan
    The measure[2] of my still renewing smart.

Yet would I not, dear Love, thou shouldst depart,   5
    But let my passions, as they first began,
    Rule, wound and please: it is thy choicest art
    To give disquiet which seems ease to man.

When all alone, I think upon thy pain,
    How thou dost travail[3] our best selves to gain: 10
    Then hourly[4] thy lessons I do learn,

Think on thy glory, which shall still ascend
    Until the world come to a final end,
    And then shall we thy lasting pow'r discern.

---

1.   Or ... or] Neither ... nor.
2.   scan / The measure] Punning on terms from metrics: analyse the metre.
3.   travail] MS reads 'traveile', and 1621 reads 'trauell'.
4.   hourly] Three syllables (MS reads 'howerly').

8.

How glow-worm-like the sun doth now appear:
   Cold beams do from his glorious face descend,
   Which shows his days and force draw to an end,
   Or that to leave-taking his time grows near.

This day his face did seem but pale, though clear;   5
   The reason is, he to the north must lend
   His light, and warmth must to that climate bend,
   Whose frozen parts could not love's heat hold dear.

Alas, if thou, bright sun, to part from hence
   Grieve so, what must I, hapless, who from thence,   10
   Where thou dost go, my blessing shall attend?

Thou shalt enjoy that sight for which I die,
   And in my heart thy fortunes do envy;
   Yet grieve; I'll love thee, for this state may end.

My muse, now happy, lay thyself to rest,
  Sleep in the quiet of a faithful love,
  Write you no more, but let the fancies move
Some other hearts; wake not to new unrest.

But if you study, be those thoughts addressed   5
  To truth, which shall eternal goodness prove,
  Enjoying of true joy, the most and best,
The endless gain which never will remove.

Leave the discourse of Venus and her son[1]
  To young beginners, and their brains inspire   10
  With stories of great love, and from that fire
Get heat to write the fortunes they have won.

And thus leave off; what's past, shows you can love,
Now let your constancy[2] your honour prove.

---

1. With motifs of Venus and her sun/son, sleep, and fire, this may look back to
    P95 and P1.
2. constancy] In *Urania*, Pamphilia becomes the embodiment of constancy.

POEMS FROM
THE COUNTESSE OF MOUNTGOMERIES URANIA

Part I

Poems are printed in the order in which they appear in *Urania*; speaker, situation and original textual location are indicated.

[U1] Unseen, unknown, I[1] here alone complain
   To rocks, to hills, to meadows and to springs,
  Which can no help return to ease my pain,
   But back my sorrows the sad echo[2] brings.
  Thus still increasing are my woes to me,   5
   Doubly resounded by that moanful voice,
  Which seems to second me in misery,
   And answer gives like friend of my own choice.
  Thus only she doth my companion prove,
   The others silently do offer ease;   10
  But those that grieve, a grieving note do love:
   Pleasures to dying eyes bring but disease;[3]
  And such am I, who daily ending live,
  Wailing a state which can no comfort give.

---

1. The shepherdess Urania speaks these lines, walking among the rocks of Pantalaria, lamenting her ignorance of her identity and parentage (Book i, page 2). She is in fact daughter of the King of Naples and sister of Amphilanthus.
2. echo] The nymph Echo pined away for love of Narcissus (Ovid, *Metamorphoses* III).
3. disease] Dis-ease, unhappiness.

[U2]   Here all alone in silence might I[1] mourn,
    But how can silence be where sorrows flow?
Sighs with complaints have poorer pains outworn,
    But broken hearts can only true grief show.

Drops of my dearest blood shall let Love know   5
    Such tears for her I shed, yet still do burn,
As no spring can quench least part of my woe,
    Till this live earth again to earth doth turn.

Hateful all thought of comfort is to me,
    Despisèd day, let me still night possess,   10
    Let me all torments feel in their excess,
    And but this light allow my state to see,

Which still doth waste, and wasting as this light[2]
Are my sad days, unto eternal night.

---

1. Written by Perissus, nephew of the King of Sicily, in love with Limena; found
   by Urania in a hidden room in a rock (i. 2–3). There is a similar situation in
   Old Arcadia, Book Three.
2. this light] A candle.

[U3]   Heart-drops distilling like a new-cut vine,
         Weep for the pains that do my [1] soul oppress,
                 Eyes do no less,
             For if you weep not, be not mine,
             Silly woes that cannot twine
                 An equal grief in such excess.   5

         You first in sorrow did begin the act,
         You saw and were the instruments of woe.
                 To let me know
             That parting would procure the fact   10
             Wherewith young hopes in bud are wracked,
                 Yet dearer eyes the rock must show,

         Which never weep, but killingly disclose
         Plagues, famine, murder in the fullest store,
                 But threaten more.   15
             This knowledge cloys my breast with woes;
             T'avoid offence my heart still chose,
                 Yet failed, and pity doth implore.

---

1. Written by Pamphilia, Queen of Pamphilia, afraid that her cousin Amphi-
   lanthus, Emperor of the Romans, may be in love with Antissia, daughter of
   the king of Romania (i. 51).

[U4]   Adieu sweet sun,
          Thy night is near,
          Which must appear
          Like mine,[1] whose light, but new begun,
          Wears as if spun   5
          By chance, not right,
          Led by a light
          False and pleasing, ever won.[2]

          Come once in view,
          Sweet heat, and light   10
          My heavy sprite
          Dulled in thy setting, made anew;
          If you renew,
          Daisies do grow
          And spring below;   15
          Blessed with thy warmth, so once I grew.

          Wilt thou return,
          Dear, bless mine eyes
          Where love's zeal lies,
          Let thy dear object mildly burn   20
          Nor fly, but turn:
          'Tis season now
          Each happy bough
          Both buds and blooms; why should I mourn?

---

1.   Sung by Steriamus, King of Albania, overheard by Amphilanthus; both are in
     love with Pamphilia (i. 54).
2.   won] The text reads 'wun'; Wroth normally spells 'wun' and 'won' as 'wunn',
     rhyming 'one' with 'alone'.

[U5]   Bear part with me,[1] most straight and pleasant tree,
        And imitate the torments of my smart
        Which cruel love doth send into my heart,
        Keep in thy skin this testament of me,

    Which love engraven hath with misery,   5
        Cutting with grief the unresisting part,
        Which would with pleasure soon have learned love's art,
        But wounds still cureless must my rulers be.

    Thy sap doth weepingly bewray[2] thy pain,
    My heart-blood drops with storms it doth sustain,   10
        Love, senseless, neither good nor mercy knows.
    Pitiless I do wound thee, while that I
    Unpitied and unthought-on, wounded cry:
        Then outlive me, and testify my woes.

---

1.   Carved by Pamphilia on an ash tree (i. 75–6). See *Old Arcadia,* Book Three, where Pamela carves a sonnet on a tree: 'Do not disdain, O straight upraised pine …' (*OA* 47).
2.   bewray] Reveal, expose.

[U6]　My[1] thoughts thou hast supported without rest,
My tired body here hath lain oppressed
With love and fear; yet be thou ever blessed;
Spring, prosper, last; I am alone unblest.

---

1. Carved by Pamphilia on the roots of the ash tree (i. 76). Pamela likewise
carved a couplet on the pine's root (*OA* 48).

[U7]   Drown me [1] not, you cruel tears,
               Which in sorrow witness bears
                   Of my wailing,
                   And love's failing.

               Floods but cover and retire,   5
               Washing faces of desire,
                   Whose fresh growing
                   Springs by flowing.

               Meadows ever yet did love
               Pleasant streams which by them move,   10
                   But your falling
                   Claims the calling

               Of a torrent curstly [2] fierce
               Past wit's power to rehearse;
                   Only crying,   15
                   Or my dying
               May instead of verse or prose
               My disastrous end disclose.

---

1.   Written by Leandrus, Prince of Achaya, in love with Pamphilia (i. 83–4).
2.   curstly] Malignantly or detestably.

[**U8**]   The sun[1] hath no long journey now to go,
            While I[2] a progress have in my desires;
            Disasters dead-low-water-like do show
            The sand, that overlooked my hoped-for hires.

            Thus I remain like one that's laid in briars,[3]   5
            Where turning brings new pain and certain woe,
            Like one, once burned, bids me avoid the fires,
            But love, true fire, will not let me be slow.

            Obedience, fear and love do all conspire
            A worthless conquest gained to ruin me,   10
            Who did but feel the height of blest desire
            When danger, doubt and loss I straight did see.
            Restless I live, consulting what to do,
            And more I study, more I still undo.

---

1. The sun] Cf. Donne's song, 'Yesternight the sun went hence, / And yet is
    here today …'.
2. Antissia's sonnet, composed in the belief that Amphilanthus has rejected her
    for Pamphilia (i. 94).
3. in briars] Cf. Wyatt's 'Sometime I fled the fire that me brent [burned] …':
    'all his labour now he laugh to scorn, / Meshed in the briars that erst was all
    to-torn'; 'in the briars' was proverbial for 'in trouble'.

[U9]   Sweet solitariness,[1] joy to those hearts
        That feel the pleasure of love's sporting darts,
        Grudge me[2] not, though a vassal to his might,
        And a poor subject to curst[3] changing's spite,
        To rest in you, or rather restless[4] move   5
        In your contents to sorrow for my love.
        A love, which living lives as dead to me,
        As holy relics which in boxes be
        Placed in a chest, that overthrows my joy,
        Shut up in change, which more than plagues destroy.   10
        These, O you solitariness, may both endure,
        And be a chirurgeon[5] to find me a cure:
        For this curst corsive[6] eating my best rest,
        Memory, sad memory in you once blessed,
        But now most miserable with the weight   15
        Of that which only shows love's strange deceit,
        You are that cruel wound that inly wears
        My soul, my body wasting into tears.
        You keep mine eyes unclosed, my heart untied,
        From letting thought of my best days to slide.   20
        Froward[7] remembrance, what delight have you
        Over my miseries to take a view?
        Why do you tell me in this same-like place
        Of earth's best blessing I have seen the face?
        But masked from me, I only see the shade   25
        Of that which once my brightest sunshine made.
        You tell me, that I then was blessed in love,
        When equal passions did together move.
        O why is this alone to bring distress
        Without a salve, but torments in excess?   30

---

1. See *Arcadia*, 'O sweet woods, the delight of solitariness …' (*OA* 34).
2. Wandering and thinking of his unhappy love, Dolorindus, King of Negro-ponte, found himself on a mount in a wood, where the sight of lovers' names carved in the trees reminded him of past happiness, causing him to think of these lines (i. 110–11).
3. curst] Malignant.
4. rest/restless] This was a popular Elizabethan word-play in drama and verse.
5. chirurgeon] Surgeon.
6. corsive] Corrosive.
7. Froward] Perverse, malevolent.

A cruel steward you are, to enroll
My once-good days, of purpose to control
With eyes of sorrow, yet leave me undone
By too much confidence, my thread so spun:
In conscience, move not such a spleen of scorn, 35
Under whose swellings my despairs are born.
Are you offended, choicest memory,
That of your perfect I did glory?
If I did so offend, yet pardon me,
Since 'twas to set forth true excellency. 40
Sufficiently I thus do punished stand,
While all that curst is, you bring to my hand.
Or, is it that I no way worthy was
In so rich treasure my few days to pass?
Alas, if so, and such a treasure given, 45
Must I for this to Hell-like pain be driven?
Fully torment me now, and what is best
Together take, and mem'ry with the rest,
Leave not that to me, since but for my ill,
Which punish may, and millions of hearts kill, 50
Then may I, lonely, sit down with my loss
Without vexation, for my losses' cross,
Forgetting pleasures late embraced with love,
Linked to a faith the world could never move,
Chained with affection I hoped could not change, 55
Not thinking earth could yield a place to range.
But staying, cruelly you set my bliss
With deepest mourning in my sight, for miss,
And thus must I imagine my curse more,
When you I loved add to my mischief's store. 60
If not, then memory continue still,
And vex me with your perfectest known skill,
While you, dear solitariness, accept
Me to your charge, whose many passions, kept
In your sweet dwellings, have this profit gained, 65
That in more delicacy none was pained.
Your rareness now receive my rarer woe
With change, and love appoints my soul to know.

[U10]   Dear Love, alas, how have I[1] wrongèd thee,
        That ceaselessly thou still dost follow me?
    My heart of diamond, clear and hard, I find
        May yet be pierced with one of the same kind
    Which hath in it engraven a love more pure   5
        Than spotless white, and deep still to endure,
    Wrought in with tears of never resting pain,
        Carved with the sharpest point of cursed disdain.
    Rain oft doth wash away a slender mark,
        Tears make mine firmer, and, as one small spark   10
    In straw may make a fire, so sparks of love
        Kindles incessantly in me to move,
    While cruellest you do only pleasure take
        To make me faster tied to scorn's sharp stake.
    'Tis harder, and more strength must usèd be,   15
        To shake a tree than boughs we bending see:
    So to move me it was alone your power,
        None else could e'er have found a yielding hour.
    Cursed be subjection, yet blessèd in this sort,
        That 'gainst all but one choice, my heart a fort   20
    Hath ever lasted: though besieged, not moved.
        But by their miss my strength the stronger proved,
    Resisting with that constant might, that win
        They scarce could parley,[2] much less get foes in.
    Yet worse than foes your slightings prove to be,   25
        When careless you no pity take on me.
    Make good my dreams, wherein you kind appear,
        Be to mine eyes, as to my soul, most dear.
    From your accustomed strangeness at last turn;
        An ancient house once fired will quickly burn   30
    And waste unhelped; my long love claims a time
        To have aid granted, to this height I climb.
    A diamond pure and hard, an unshaked tree,
        A burning house find, help, and prize in me.

---

1. Composed by Pamphilia during a solitary early morning walk in the forest
    (i. 121).
2. win ... parley] They could scarcely negotiate a conquest.

[U11]   Stay mine [1] eyes, these floods of tears
          Seems but follies weakly growing,
      Babes at nurse such wailing bears,
          Frowardness such drops bestowing:
      But Niobe must show my fate,   5
      She wept and grieved herself a state. [2]

      My sorrows like her babes appear
          Daily added by increasing;
      She lost them, I lose my dear,
          Not one spared from woes ne'er ceasing: 10
      She made a rock, heaven drops down tears,
      Which pity shows, and on her wears.

---

1.   Song ('or rather part of one') sung by Antissia in the garden woods, after her previous conversation with Pamphilia (i. 122).
2.   Niobe's grief at the death of her children turned her to a stone statue (Ovid, *Metamorphoses* VI).

[U12]   Sh: Dear,[1] how do thy winning eyes
                  my senses wholly tie?
        She: Sense of sight, wherein most lies
                  change, and variety.
        Sh: Change in me?   5
        She: Choice in thee some new delights to try.
        Sh: When I change, or choose but thee,
                  then changèd be mine eyes.
        She: When you, absent, see not me,
                  will you not break these ties?   10
        Sh: How can I
                  ever fly where such perfection lies?
        She: I must yet more try thy love:
                  how if that I should change?
        Sh: In thy heart can never move   15
                  a thought so ill, so strange.
        She: Say I die?
        Sh: Never I could from thy love estrange.
        She: Dead, what canst thou love in me,
                  when hope, with life, is fled?   20
        Sh: Virtue, beauty, faith in thee,
                  which live will, though thou dead.
        She: Beauty dies.
        Sh: Not where lies a mind so richly sped.
        She: Thou dost speak so fair, so kind,   25
                  I cannot choose but trust.
        Sh: None unto so chaste a mind
                  should ever be unjust.
        She: Then thus rest,
                  true possessed of love without mistrust.

---

1. Pamphilia and Amphilanthus arrive at the Throne of Love, on Cyprus, and
    liberate lovers trapped by enchantment, to celebrate which the King of
    Cyprus has his shepherds and shepherdesses present songs (i. 143). *RS* has
    a comparable faith-testing shepherds' dialogue (*RS* 6, 'Shepherd, i' faith,
    now say how well …').

Love what art thou? A vain thought
   In our minds by fancy wrought;
   Idle smiles did thee beget,
   While fond wishes made the net
   Which so many fools have caught.   5

Love what art thou? Light and fair,
   Fresh as morning, clear as th'air,
   But too soon thy evening change
   Makes thy worth with coldness range,
   Still thy joy is mixed with care.   10

Love what art thou? A sweet flower,
   Once full blown, dead in an hour,
   Dust in wind as staid remains
   As thy pleasure or our gains,
   If thy humour change to lour.[2]   15

Love what art thou? Childish, vain,
   Firm as bubbles made by rain,
   Wantonness thy greatest pride:
   These foul faults thy virtues hide,
   But babes can no staidness gain.   20

Love what art thou? Causeless cursed,
   Yet alas, these not the worst,
   Much more of thee may be said,
   But thy law I once obeyed,
   Therefore say no more at first.   25

---

1. The next song, by a shepherdess (i. 144).
2. lour] Gloom, storm.

[U14]   Who can blame me if I [1] love?
Since Love before the world did move.
When I loved not, I despaired,
Scarce for handsomeness I cared.
Since, so much I am refined   5
As new framed of state and mind,
    Who can blame me if I love,
    Since Love [2] before the world did move.

    Some, in truth of love beguiled,
      Have him blind and childish styled,   10
      But let none in these persist,
      Since so judging judgement missed,
      Who can blame me?

    Love in Chaos [3] did appear,
      When nothing was, yet he seemed clear,   15
      Nor when light could be descried,
      To his crown a light was tied.
      Who can blame me?

    Love is truth, and does delight
      Where as honour shines most bright;   20
      Reason's self doth love approve,
      Which makes us ourselves to love.
      Who can blame me?

    Could I my past time begin,
      I would not commit such sin   25
      To live an hour and not to love,
      Since love makes us perfect prove.
      Who can blame me?

---

1.   Sung by a shepherd in response to Amphilanthus's criticism of the previous
     mocking treatment of love (i. 144–5). The last song in the first book.
2.   Love] Here seen as a divine, creative force.
3.   chaos] Primordial matter, out of which the order of the universe was created.

[U15]   Pray thee Diana, tell me,[1] is it ill,
        as some do say thou think'st it is, to love?
    Methinks thou pleasèd art with what I prove,
        since joyful light thy dwelling still doth fill.

    Thou seemst not angry, but with cheerful smiles   5
        beholdst my passions; chaste indeed thy face
    Doth seem, and so doth shine with glorious grace;
        for other loves the trust of Love beguiles.

    Be bright then still, most chaste and clearest Queen,
        shine on my torments with a pitying eye: 10
    Thy coldness can but my despairs descry,
        and my faith by thy clearness better seem.

    Let those have heat that dally in the sun,
        I scarce have known a warmer state than shade,
    Yet hottest beams of zeal have purely made   15
        my self an off'ring burnt, as I was won.

    Once sacrificed, but ashes can remain,
        which in an ivory box of truth enclose
    The innocency whence my ruins flows:
        accept them as thine, 'tis a chaste love's gain.   20

---

1.   Steriamus's response to his mistress's rejection, while looking at the moon
    (Diana is both the moon and the goddess of chastity) (ii. 152).

[U16] Tears sometimes flow from mirth as well as sorrow;
Pardon me then, if I[1] again do borrow
Of thy moist rine[2] some smiling drops, approving[3]
Joy for true joy, which now proceeds from loving.

---

1. Pamphilia's addition to the poem she carved on the ash tree [U5] (ii.161).
2. rine] Bark of the tree.
3. approving] Displaying.

[U17] How do I[1] find my soul's extremest anguish
        With restless care my heart's eternal languish?
      Torments in life increasing still with anguish,
        Unquiet sleeps which breed my senses' languish.
      Hope yet appears, which somewhat helps my anguish,   5
        And lends a spark of life to salve this languish,
      Breath to desire, and ease to foregone anguish,
        Balms but not cures to bitter tasting languish.
      Yet straight I feel hope proves but greater anguish,
        False in itself, to me brings cruel languish.   10
      Could I not hope, I suffer might my anguish,
        At least with lesser torture, smart and languish.
      For rebel hope, I see thy smiles are anguish,
        Both Prince and subject of e'erlasting languish.

---

1. Philarchos, youngest son of the King of Morea, sings this, overheard by
    Nereana (unhappily in love with Steriamus) while lost in the woods (ii. 166–7).

[U18]   Gone is my[1] joy, while here I mourn
               In pains of absence, and of care;
          The heav'ns for my sad griefs do turn
               Their face to storms, and show despair.

          The days are dark, the nights oppressed,   5
               With cloud'ly weeping for my pain,
          Which in their acting seem distressed,
               Sighing like grief for absent gain.

          The sun gives place, and hides his face,
               That day can now be hardly known,   10
          Nor will the stars in night yield grace
               To sun-robbed heav'n by woe o'erthrown.

          Our light is fire in fearful flames,
               The air tempestuous blasts of wind;
          For warmth, we have forgot those names,   15
               Such blasts and storms are us assigned.

          And still you blessed heav'ns, remain
               Distempered while this cursed pow'r
          Of absence rules, which brings my pain,
               Let your care be more still to lour.   20

          But when my sun doth back return,
               Call yours again to lend his light,
          That they in flames of joy may burn,
               Both equal shining in our sight.

---

1. Pamphilia thinks of this song while walking alone in the garden (ii. 177).

[U19]   When I [1] with trembling ask if you love still,
        My soul afflicted lest I give offence,
        Though sensibly discerning my worst ill,
        Yet rather than offend, with grief dispense,

    Faintly you say, you must; poor recompense,   5
        When grateful love is fore. [2] I see the hill
        Which mars my prospect [3] love, and Oh from thence
        I taste and take of loss the poisoned pill.

    While one coal lives, the rest dead all about
        That still is fire: so your love, now burned out,   10
        Tells what you were, though to deceiving led.

    The sun in summer and in winter shows
        Like [4] bright, but not like hot, fair false-made blows;
        You shine on me, but your love's heat is dead.

---

1. Composed by the shepherdess Allarina in the hope of regaining her beloved
    (ii. 186).
2. fore] Present.
3. prospect] Visible, in view.
4. Like] Equally bright but not equally hot, deceptively fine weather.

[U20]   You pow'rs divine of love-commanding eyes,
      Within whose lids are kept the fires of love,
    Close not yourselves to ruin me,[1] who lies
      In bands of death, while you in darkness move.

    One look doth give a spark to kindle flames   5
      To burn my heart, a martyr to your might;
    Receiving one kind smile, I find new frames
      For love to build me wholly to your light.

    My soul doth fix all thoughts upon your will,
      Gazing unto amazement, greedy how   10
    To see those blessèd lights of love's heav'n bow
      Themselves on wretchèd me, who else they kill.

    You then that rule love's god, in mercy flourish:
    Gods must not murder, but their creatures nourish.

---

1.   Sung for Pamphilia by the shepherd Alanius, in love with Liana (ii. 212).

[U21]   You pure and holy fire,[1]
        Which kindly now will not aspire[2]
        To hot performance of your nature, turn
        Cross to yourself and never burn
        These relics of a blessèd hand,   5
        Joined with mutual holy band
        Of love and dear desire.

Blame me not, dearest lines,
        That with love's flames your blackness twines,
        My heart more mourning doth for you express,   10
        But grief for sorrow is no less.
        Deepest groans can cover, not change, woe,
        Heart's the tomb, keeps in the show
        Which worth from ill refines.

Alas yet as you burn,   15
        My pity smarts, and groans to turn
        Your pains away, and yet you must consume
        Content in me, must bear no plume;
        Dust-like despair may with me live,
        Yet shall your memory out-drive   20
        These pains wherein I mourn.

You relics of pure love,
        To sacred keep with me remove,
        Purged by this fire from harm and jealous fear,
        To live with me both chaste and clear,   25
        The true preserveress of pure truths,
        Who to your grave gives a youth
        In faith to live and move.

Famous bodies still in flames
        Did anciently preserve their names;   30
        Unto this funeral nobly you are come,
        Honour giving you this tomb.
        Tears and love, perform your rites,
        To which constancy bears lights
        To burn, and keep from blame.   35

---

1. Composed by Melasinda, Queen of Hungary, after burning a letter from her
    suitor Ollorandus, King of Bohemia, and putting the ashes in her cabinet (the
    'sacred keep') (ii. 227–8).
2. See *RS* 13: 'My soul in purest fire / Doth not aspire / To reward of my pain …'.

[U22]　　　　Love peruse me,[1] seek and find
　　　　　　How each corner of my mind
　　　　　　　　is a twine[2]
　　　　　　　　woven to shine,
　　　　　　Not a web[3] ill-made, foul-framed,　　　　　5
　　　　　　Bastard not by father named:
　　　　　　　　such in me
　　　　　　　　cannot be.
　　　　　　Dear, behold me, you shall see
　　　　　　Faith the hive and Love the bee,　　　　　10
　　　　　　　　which do bring
　　　　　　　　gain and sting.
　　　　　　Pray dissect me, sinews, veins
　　　　　　Hold, and love's life in those gains
　　　　　　　　lying bare　　　　　15
　　　　　　　　to despair,
　　　　　　When you thus anatomise[4]
　　　　　　All my body, my heart prise,[5]
　　　　　　　　being true
　　　　　　　　just to you.　　　　　20
　　　　　　Close the trunk, embalm the chest,
　　　　　　Where your power still shall rest;
　　　　　　　　Joy entomb,
　　　　　　　　Love's just doom.

---

1. Sung by a love-lorn maiden fishing by a stream, overheard by Amphilanthus and Ollorandus (ii. 241).
2. twine] Thread; one contemporary theory was that the body is held in order by threads of sinews or nerves emanating from the brain to every part. She may also have in mind the fishing-line.
3. web] Fabric for weaving, in a frame; may also be a fishing-net.
4. Cf. Donne's 'Love's Exchange', 40–3: 'Kill, and dissect me, Love; for this / Torture against thine own end is, / Racked carcases make ill anatomies'.
5. prise] Prise open; a possible play on 'prize'.

[U23] From victory in love I[1] now am come
   Like a commander killed at the last blow:
   Instead of laurel, to obtain a tomb,
   With triumph that a steely faith I show.
   Here must my grave be, which I thus will frame,   5
   Made of my stony heart, to other name
   Than what I honour; scorn brings me my tomb;
   Disdain the priest to bury me, I come.

  Clothed in the relics of a spotless love,
   Embrace me, you that let true lovers in;   10
   Pure fires of truth do light me when I move,
   Which lamp-like last, as if they did begin.
   On you, the sacred tomb of love, I lay
   My life, neglect sends to the hellish way,
   As off'ring of the chastest soul that knew   15
   Love and his blessing, till a change both slew.

  Here do I sacrifice world's time of truth,
   Which only death can let me part withal;
   Though in my dying, have perpetual youth
   Buried alone in you, whereby I fall.   20
   Open the graves where lovers' saints have lain,
   See if they will not fill themselves with pain
   Of my affliction, or strive for my place,
   Who with a constant honour gain this grace.

  Burn not my body yet, unless an urn   25
   Be framed, of equal virtue with my love,
   To hold the ashes which, though pale, will burn
   In true love's embers, where he still will move;
   And by no means let my dust fall to earth,
   Lest men do envy this my second birth,   30
   Or learn by it to find a better state
   Than I could do for love immaculate.

---

1. Composed by Emilena, Princess of Styria, on being betrayed by a man she
  believes to be Amphilanthus, and sung by one of her maids (ii. 249–50).

Thus here, O here's my resting place ordained:
    Fate made it ere I was. I not complain,
    Since had I kept, I had but bliss obtained,   35
    And such for loyalty I sure shall gain.
    Fame bears the torches for my last farewell
    To life, but not to love, for there I dwell;
    But to that place, neglect appoints for tomb
    Of all my hopes; thus Death I come, I come.   40

[U24]   I, who do feel the highest part of grief,
          shall I be left without relief?[1]
    I, who for you do cruel torments bear,
          will you, alas, leave me in fear?
    Know, comfort never could more welcome be   5
          than in this needful time to me,
    One drop of comfort will be higher prized
          than seas of joys, if once despised;
    Turn not the tortures which for you I try
          upon my heart, to make me die.   10
    Have I offended? 'twas at your desire,
          when by your vows you felt love's fire;
    What I did err in, was to please your will:
          can you get, and the offspring kill?
    The greatest fault which I committed have   15
          is, you did ask, I freely gave.
    Kindly relent, let causeless curstness fly,
          give but one sigh, I blest shall die;
    But O you cannot, I have much displeased,
          striving to gain, I loss have seized.   20
    My state I see, and you your ends have gained,
          I'm lost, since you have me obtained
    And since I cannot please your first desire,
          I'll blow and nourish scorner's fire.
    As salamanders in the fire do live,   25
          so shall those flames my being give,
    And though against your will I live and move,
          forsaken creatures live and love.
    Do you proceed, and you may well confess
          you wronged my care, while I care less.   30

---

1.   Antissia realizes that Amphilanthus loves Pamphilia rather than her (ii. 271–2).

[U25] Blame me not, dearest,[1] though grievèd for your sake.
    Love, mild to you, on me triumphing sits,
    Sifting the choicest ashes of my wits
    Burnt like a phoenix, change but such could shake.

And a new heat, given by your eyes, did make   5
    Embers, dead cold, call spirits from the pits
    Of dark despair to favour new-felt fits,
    And as from death to this new choice to wake.

Love thus crowns you with power: scorn not the flames,
    Though not the first, yet which as purely rise   10
    As the best light, which sets unto our eyes,
    And then again ascends free from all blames.

Pureness is not alone in one fixed place:
Who dies to live, finds change a happy grace.

---

1. After the disappointments experienced by Urania and Steriamus in their first
loves, they found happiness with each other and married; here he defends 'a
second love' (ii. 276).

[U26]   Love among the clouds did hover
        Seeking where to find a lover: [1]
        In the Court he none could find,
        Towns too mean were in that kind,
        At last as he was ripe to crying,   5
        In forest woods he found one lying.

    Underneath a tree fast sleeping,
        Sprit [2] of Love her body keeping,
        Where the soul of Cupid lay
        Though he higher then did stay,   10
        When he himself in her descrying,
        He hasted more then with his flying.

    And his tender hand soft laying
        On her breast his fires were playing,
        Waked her with his baby game.   15
        She who knew love was no shame,
        With his new sport smiled as delighted,
        And homeward went by Cupid lighted.

    See the shady woods bestowing
        That which none can ask as owing,   20
        But in courts where plenties flow,
        Love doth seldom pay, but owe.
        Then still give me this country pleasure,
        Where sweet love chastely keeps his treasure.

---

1. An earl's son, posing as a country swain, sings this seduction song to a forest
    nymph (iii. 294–5).
2. sprit] Spirit.

[**U27**]   Infernal spirits[1] listen to my moans,
        From cavy depths, give hearing to my groans
        Great Pluto,[2] let thy sad abiding[3] move
        With hellish fires, to flame for fires of love;
        Let Charon[4] pass my woes unto thine ears;   5
        His boat, if empty, they shall load it well
        With tortures great as are the pains of hell,
        And weightier than the earth this body bears.

    Take down my spirit, cloyed with grief and pain,
        Conjure the darkest pits to let me gain   10
        Some corner for a rest; if not, let me,
        O Pluto, wander and complain to thee:
        No corsive can make wounds have torture more,
        Nor this disfavour vex a forlorn soul
        (If all thy furies were put in a roll)   15
        Than love gives me; ah bitter eating sore.

    Call thy great council, and afflicted sp'rits,
        Examine well their woes, with all their nights,
        And you shall find none there that are not mine,
        Nay, my least with their greatest jointly twine.   20
        Let saddest echo from her hollow cave
        Answer the horrid plaints my sorrow gives,
        Which in like mournful and vast cavern lives:
        Then judge the murdering passions which I have.

    My judge is deaf, then, O thy justice prove,   25
        Mend thou the fault of proud forgetful love,
        Release me from thy court, and send me out
        Unto thy brother Jove, whose love and doubt
        Hath oft transformed him from his heavenly kind:
        So now from thee transform my killing care   30
        To blessing, and from hell into the air:
        Dark grief should not a loving fancy bind.

---

1. The daughter of Plamergus, lamenting the death of her lover Polydorus, reads
    this aloud in her tomb of red marble, where she dies (iii. 303).
2. Pluto] The god of the underworld.
3. abiding] Dwelling-place.
4. Charon] Ferried the shades of the dead across the River Styx into the
    underworld.

[**U28**]   The joy you say[1] the heavens in motion try
　　　　Is not for change, but for their constancy.
　　Should they stand still, their change you then might move,
　　　　And serve your turn in praise of fickle love.
　　That pleasure is not but diversified,　　　　　　　　　5
　　　　Plainly makes proof your youth, not judgement tried.
　　The sun's renewing course yet is not new,
　　　　Since 'tis but one set course he doth pursue,
　　And though it feignèd be that he hath changed,
　　　　'Twas when he from his royal seat hath ranged:　　10
　　His glorious splendour, free from such a stain,
　　　　Was forced to take new shapes, his end to gain.
　　And thus indeed the sun may give you leave
　　　　To take his worst part, your best to deceive.
　　And whereof he himself hath been ashamed,　　　　15
　　　　Your greatness praiseth, fitter to be blamed
　　Nothing in greatness loves a strange delight,
　　　　Should we be governed then by appetite,
　　A hungry humour, surfeiting on ill,
　　　　Which glutton-like with cramming will not fill.　　20
　　No serpent can bring forth so foul a birth
　　　　As change in love, the hatefull'st thing on earth;
　　Yet you do venture this vice to commend
　　　　As if of it you patron were, or friend:
　　Foster it still, and you shall true man be　　　　　　25
　　　　Who first for change lost his felicity.
　　Rivers, 'tis true, are clearest when they run,
　　　　But not because they have new places won,
　　For if the ground be muddy where they fall,
　　　　The clearness, with their change, doth change withal;　30
　　Lakes may be sweet if so their bottoms be;
　　　　From roots, not from the leaves, our fruit we see.
　　But love too rich a prize is for your share;
　　　　Some little idle liking he can spare
　　Your wit to play withal; but true love must　　　　35
　　　　Have truer hearts to lodge in, and more just,
　　While this may be allowed you for love's might,
　　　　As for day's glory framèd was the night.

1.　The response of Polydorus's wife to the would-be usurper Nicholarus, who
　　had praised variety in love (iii. 318–19).

That you can outward fairness so affect
    Shows that the worthier part you still neglect,   40
Or else your many changings best appears,
    For beauty changeth faster than the years;
And that you can love greatness makes it known,
    The want of height in goodness of your own.
'Twas not a happiness in ancient time   45
    To hold plurality to be no crime,
But a mere ignorance, which they did mend
    When the true light did glorious lustre lend.
And much I wonder you will highly rate
    The brutish love of nature, from which state   50
Reason doth guide us, and doth difference make
    From sensual will, true reason's laws to take.
Were't not for reason, we but brutish were,
    Nor from the beasts did we at all differ;
Yet these you praise, the true style, opinion,   55
    By which truth's government is shrewdly[1] gone.
Honour by you esteemed a title true,[2]
    A title cannot claimed by change as due;
It is too high for such low worth to reach,
    Heav'n gifts bestow'th as to belong to each.[3]   60
And this, true love must in revenge bestow
    On you, his sacred pow'r with pain to know:
A love to give you, fickle, loose and vain,
    Yet you, with ceaseless grief, seek to obtain
Her fleeting favours, while you, wailing, prove,   65
    Merely for punishment, a steady love:
Let her be fair, but false, great, disdainful,
    Chaste but to you, to all others gainful;
Then shall your liberty and choice be tied
    To pain, repentance and (the worst sin) pride.   70
But if this cannot teach you how to love,
    Change still, till you can better counsel prove:
Yet be assured, while these conceits you have,
    Love will not own one shot (you say) he gave.

---

1. shrewdly] Grievously, to bad effect.
2. A title that cannot be claimed as due as a result of change.
3. Heaven bestows gifts that are appropriate to each recipient.

His are all true, all worthy, yours unjust;   75
    Then (changing you), what can you from him trust?[1]
Repentance true-felt oft the gods doth win,
    Then, in your wane of love,[2] leave this foul sin:
So shall you purchase favour, banish shame,
    And with some care obtain a lover's name.   80

---

1. trust] Expect to receive.
2. wane of love] Deficiency of true love.

[U29] As these drops fall, so hope now drops on me,[1]
　　sparingly, cool, yet much more than of late,
　　as with despair I changèd had a state,
　　yet not possessed, govern but modestly.[2]

　　Dearest, let these drops heav'nly showers prove,　　　5
　　　and but the sea fit to receive thy streams,
　　　in multitudes compare but with sun beams,
　　　and make sweet mixture, 'twixt them and thy love.

　　The sea's rich plenty joined to our delights,
　　　the sun's kind warmth unto thy pleasing smiles,　　10
　　　when wisest hearts thy love-make eyes beguiles,
　　　and, vassal, brings to them the greatest sprites.

　　Rain on me rather than be dry; I gain
　　　nothing so much as by such harmless tears,
　　　which take away the pains of loving fears,　　　15
　　　and finely wins an everlasting reign.

　　But if like heat-drops[3] you do waste away,
　　　glad, as disburdened of a hot desire,
　　　let me be rather lost, perish in fire,
　　　than by those hopeful signs brought to decay.　　20

　　Sweet, be a lover pure and permanent,
　　　cast off gay clothes of change, and such false sleights:[4]
　　　love is not love but where truth has her rights,
　　　else, like boughs from the perfect body rent.

---

1. Bellamira, regaining hope of the King of Dalmatia, wrote this while sitting in
　an orchard as rain-drops began to fall (iii. 336-7).
2. Governing a state with some restraint, not having taken full possession of it.
3. heat-drops] A few drops of rain ushering in a hot day.
4. sleights] Tricks or deceptions; the text reads 'slights', which would mean
　'contemptuous treatment'.

[U30]   You,[1] who never ending saw
                Of pleasure's best delighting,
            You that cannot wish a thaw,
                Who feels no frost of spiting,
            Keeping Cupid's hand in awe,   5
                That sees but by your lighting,
            Be not still too cruel bent
                Against a soul distressed,
            Whose heart love long since hath rent
                And pitiless oppressed: 10
            But let malice now be spent,
                And former ills redressed.
            Grieve I do for what is past,
                Let favour then be granted;
            Thieves, by judgement to die cast,   15
                Have not of mercy wanted,
            But alone at feasts I fast,
                As thief, of pleasure scanted:
            You accuse me that I stole
                From you your heart's directing,   20
            All your thoughts at my control,
                Yet passions still rejecting;
            But you place me in the roll
                Of left-loves new electing.[2]
            Though I kinder was to it,   25
                My heart in place bestowing,
            To make room for yours more fit,
                As just exchange, truth flowing,
            Till you fondly gained the bit,[3]
                And flying, left love owing.   30
            Which debt resting still unpaid,
                Let this at last be gained,
            When your new loves have you stayed,[4]
                With welcome choice obtained:
            Let change on your breast be laid,   35
                While I live still unstained.

---

1. Searching for his wife Urania, Steriamus mistakes her for Lady Pastora, who,
    dressed as a shepherdess, sings as she combs her hair (iii. 355–6).
2. The list of those who have left former loves and chosen new.
3. gained the bit] For a horse to take the bit in its teeth is for it to become
    uncontrollable.   4. stayed] Satisfied.

[U31] Cruel Remembrance, alas now be still,
          Put me not on the rack to torture me:[1]
       I do confess my greatest misery
          Lives in your plenty, my last harm your skill.

       Poison and venom only once do kill,   5
          While you perpetually new mischiefs see,
       To vex my soul with endless memory,
          Leaving no thought that may increase my ill.

       Else have you need to tell me I was blest,
          Rich in the treasure of content and love,   10
       When I like him or her had sweetest rest
          But passed like days, you stay, and vexings prove.

       Changed from all favours, you add unto despair:
       Who under these weights groan, most wretched are.

---

1. Pamphilia fears that Amphilanthus has left her for another woman (iii. 390).

Unquiet grief, search further in my heart:
    If place be found which thou hast not possessed,
    Or so much space can build hope's smallest nest,
    Take it, 'tis thine, mine is the lodge of smart.

Despair, despair hath used the skilfull'st art   5
    To ruin hope, and murder easeful rest:
    O me, despair my vine of hope hath pressed,
    Ravished the grapes, the leaves left for my part.

Yet ruler grief, not thou despair deny,
    This last request proclaims 'twas not suspect[2]   10
    Grafted this bud of sorrow in my breast,

But knowledge daily doth my loss descry.
    Cold love's now matched with care, change with respect:[3]
    When true flames lived, these false fires were suppressed.

---

1. Pamphilia unwillingly reads some of her verse to Meriana, Queen of Macedon: 'I seldom make any but sonnets, and they are not so sweet in rehearsing as others that come more roundly off' (iii. 392).
2. suspect] Suspicion.
3. respect] Careful attention, caution.

[U33]   Loss, my [1] molester, at last patient be,
        And satisfied with thy curst self, or move
        Thy mournful force thus oft on perjured love,
        To waste a life which lives by mischief's fee.[2]

    Who will behold true misery, view me,   5
        And find, what wit hath feigned, I fully prove:
        A heaven-like blessing changed, thrown from above
        Into despair, whose worst ill I do see.

    Had I not happy been, I had not known
        So great a loss; a king deposed, feels most   10
        The torment of a throne-like want, when lost,
        And up must look to what late was his own.

    Lucifer down cast, his loss doth grieve:
        My Paradise of joy gone, do I live?

---

1. Pamphilia reads this while waiting by a stream for the nymph Silviana, who
    has vowed herself to Diana (chastity). After the poem, she answers her own
    question: 'Yes I do live,' cried she, 'but to what end? Only to mourn, lament
    and moan a state all pity wants' (iii. 409).
2. by ... fee] Subject to.

[U34]   O that I [1] might but now as senseless be
           Of my felt pains, as is that pleasant tree
           Of the sweet music thou, dear bird, dost make,
           Who I imagine doth my woes partake.
           Yet contrary we do our passions move,   5
           Since in sweet notes thou dost thy sorrows prove.
           I but in sighs and tears can show I grieve,
           And those best spent, if worth do them believe;
           Yet thy sweet pleasure makes me ever find
           That happiness to me, as love, is blind,   10
           And these thy wrongs in sweetness to attire
           Throws down my hopes, to make my woes aspire.
           Besides, of me th'advantage thou hast got,
           Thy grief thou utter'st, mine I utter not,
           Yet thus at last we may agree in one,   15
           I mourn for what still is, thou, what is gone. [2]

---

1.   Sitting in a grove, the Queen of Naples (possibly based on Mary Sidney, Coun-
     tess of Pembroke) writes this when she hears a nightingale singing (iii. 416).
2.   one/gone] A good rhyme (rhyming with 'own').

[U35] Dear, though unconstant, these I[1] send to you
  As witnesses, that still my love is true.
  Receive these lines as images of death,
  That bear the infants of my latest breath,
  And to my triumph, though I die in woe,   5
  With welcome glory, since you will it so;
  Especially my ending is the less,
  When I examples see of my distress.
  As Dido,[2] one whose misery was had
  By love, for which she in death's robes was clad; 10
  Yet lost she less than I, for I possessed
  And love enjoyed, she liked what was professed;
  Most cruel, and the death-lik'st kind of ill,
  To lose the blessing of contentment's will.
  Fair Ariadne never took more care   15
  Than I did how you might in safety fare,
  Her thread, my life was, to draw you from harm,
  My study, wholly how I might all charm
  That dangerous were, while pleasures you obtained,
  And I the hazard with the honour gained: 20
  Yet she this his life saved, he her honour lost;
  That false prince Theseus flying, left her crossed
  With his abandoning her truth and love,
  Leaving her desolate, alone to prove
  His love, or ended or but giv'n for need,[3]   25
  Caused her with misery to gain that meed.[4]
  I Ariadne am alike oppressed,
  Alike deserving, and alike distressed.
  Ungrateful Demophon to Phyllis fair,
  A Thracian lady, caused by[5] like despair   30

---

1. Composed by Dorolina after her lover betrayed her; despite her warning that 'the verses are long and tedious', her audience insisted on her recital of famous women deceived by men (iii. 418–20).

2. Dido] Dido, Ariadne, Phyllis, Medea and Penelope were all betrayed (by Aeneas, Theseus, Demophon, Jason and Ulysses, respectively); the stories were well known from various sources, including Ovid's *Heroides*.

3. prove … need] To discover that his love was either ended or given only from necessity.

4. meed] Recompense.

5. 'by' is redundant to the sense.

Or greater far, for after fervent love,
In which blest time he freely still did prove
What is desired or loved, he left this queen
And bliss for a less kingdom, which had been
Before his father's, and by reason right,[1]   35
For Theseus was his sire, that king of spite.
Thus did he both inherit state and ill,
While Phyllis self her lovely self did kill,
Making a tree her throne, a cord the end
Of her affections, which his shame did send.   40
I strangled am, with your unkindness choked,
While cruelty is with occasions[2] cloaked.
Medea witch, with her enchanting skill
Did purchase what was craved by her will,
Yet was by Jason left at last, which shows   45
Love only free from all bewitching blows
But his own witchcraft, which is worst of ills,
Never absenting till all joy it spills.
Charms, it may be, with-held you now from me:
Break through them, leave that Circe so oft free,   50
The sirens' song, Calypso's sweet delights,
And look on faith, which light is of true lights.
Turn back the eyes of your changed heart, and see
How much you sought, how fondly once sought me.
What travail[3] did you take to win my love,   55
How did you sue that I as kind would prove!
This is forgot as yesterday's liked sport,
Love winning lasting long, once won proves short.
I like Penelope, have all this time
Of your absenting, let no thought to climb   60
In me of change, though courted, and pursued
By love, persuasions, and even fashions rude
Almost to force extending, yet still she
Continued constant, and as I am free.
Ten years a cause was for Ulysses' stay   65
While Troy besiegèd was, but then away

---

1. by reason right] With good cause.
2. occasions] Excuses, pretexts.
3. travail] Text reads 'travell'; the pun was common, and here perhaps alludes
    to the wanderings of Ulysses.

Was homeward bent by all, save him who stayed,
And ten years more on foreign beauties preyed.
Against his will,[1] he oft his will enjoyed,
And with variety at last was cloyed.   70
Change wearied him, when weary he returned,
And from his wand'ring then to staidness turned.
Come you now back, I thus invite you home,
And love you, as if you did never roam:
I have forgot it as if never done,   75
And do but think me anew to be won.
I shall appear, it may be, as I did,
And all past faults shall in my breast be hid;
Try me again, and you shall truly find,
Where fairness wanteth, clearness of a mind;   80
Fairer and richer than the mass of all
Their persons which from me have made you fall,
If joined together, and from thence to frame
A mind of beauteous faith, fit for the name
Of worthy constancy, enriched with truth,   85
Which gave me to you, and so held my youth
In young desires, still growing to your love:
Nourish them now, and let me your love prove.
Leave the new powerful charms of strangers' tongues,
Which always truth with their fair falsehood wrongs.   90
Come back to me, who never knew the plot
To cross your mind, or to thy will a not:[2]
Come, I say, come again, and with Ulysses
Enjoy the blessings of your best blisses;
Happy the comfort of a chaste love's bed,   95
Blessèd the pillow that upholds the head
Of loyal loving, shame's the other's due,
Leave those for me who cannot but be true.
Come, and give life, or in your stay[3] send death
To her that lives in you, else draws no breath.   100

---

1. will] A play on different senses of 'will', as intention and as sexual appetite.
2. a not] Text reads 'an nott', i.e. 'how to oppose'; 'knot' might also make sense.
3. in your stay] By staying away.

[U36]   Why do you so much wish for rain, when I,[1]
        Whose eyes still show'ring are, stand you so nigh?
        Think you that my poor eyes now cannot lend
        You store enough? Alas, but rightly bend
        Your looks on me, and you shall see a store   5
        Able to moisten earth, and ten earths more,
        Sighs to make Heaven as soft as tender wool,
        And grief sufficient to make up the full
        Of all despairs; then wish not, since in me
        Containèd are tears, grief, and misery.   10

---

1.   Musalina, one of Amphilanthus's lovers, returns home to find Romania suffering from drought and everyone wanting rain, and writes this to express her sorrow on leaving him (iii. 423).

Pamphilia tells the story of Lindamira (a possible anagram of Ladi Mari), married but in love with another, as a result of which she is banished from the court: '[Her] complaint, because I lik't it, or rather found her estate so neere agree with mine, I put into Sonnets.' The next seven sonnets constitute a separate sequence expressing grief at rejection and exile. (iii. 426–8). In *Old Arcadia*, Book Four, Philisides writes love poems to 'Mira'.

[U37] 1.

Dear eyes farewell, my sun once, now my end;[1]
　　While your kind willing grace I felt, all joy
　　In soul I knew withdrawn, you now destroy[2]
　　The house that being gave to love's best friend.

You now, alas, to other objects bend　　　　　　　5
　　That warmth of bliss which best delights enjoy;
　　Striving to win an oft-won idle toy,
　　By falsehood nursed, such creatures seldom mend.

Try your new loves, affect the choice of store,
　　And be assured, they likewise will choose more,　　10
　　Which I yet grieve; for though the loss I bear,

I would have none with you to challenge right;
　　But bear you must, for making choice so light:
　　Yet still your beams I'll love, shine you elsewhere.[3]

---

1. iii, 426.
2. While I once felt your grace, now the joy I knew has been withdrawn, and you destroy me.
3. Even though you shine elsewhere, I'll still love your beams.

O deadly rancour to a constant heart: [1]
Frowns and neglect, my only favours be;
Sometimes a cold respect is granted me,
But hot flames to those eyes joy in my smart. [2]

Once yet, for justice' sake, weigh my hard part: 5
In gratefulness I should kind usage see,
For being tied alone to you, else free,
Till by your wrongs now joined with heart-broke smart.

A glorious triumph you no doubt shall have
To crown your victory on murder's grave,   10
While falsehood bears the arms my life hath won.

I only twice seven years' love shall gain [3]
Change, worse than absence, or death's cruellest pain:
The last yet got, you have your labour done.

---

1. iii. 426.
2. hot flames ... eyes] Warm encouragement to those whose eyes ...
3. The Queen banished Lindamira, after fourteen years' service and 'unchanged
    affection', as a result of rumours: 'Despite fourteen years' love, I shall suffer
    your change of affection, which is worse than absence ...'.

A surgeon I would ask, but 'tis too late [1]
   To stay the bleeding wound of my hurt heart:
   The root is touched, and the last drops depart,
   As weeping for succeeding others' fate.

Alas, that my killed heart should wail my state,   5
   Or leisure have to think on aught but smart,
   Nor doth it but with pity bear a part,
   With her embraced yours like a loving mate. [2]

But now unmarried by a new disdain,
   Cold death must take the body from her love,   10
   And thou, poor heart, must end for my unworth. [3]

Conscience is lost, and outward fairness gains
   The place where worth did, or else seemed to, move:
   Thus world, like change, new trial still brings forth.

---

1.   iii. 426–7.
2.   Lindamira's heart once embraced the beloved's.
3.   unworth] Possibly (as in 1.13) a play on 'Wroth', here producing a kind of self-cancellation.

O memory, could I but lose thee now,[1]
  At least learn to forget as I did move
  My best and only thoughts to wait on love,[2]
  And be as registers of my made vow.

Could I but let my mind to reason bow,   5
  Or see plain wrongs, neglects and slightings prove
  In that dear sphere[3] which as the Heav'ns above
  I prized, and homage to it did allow.

Canst thou not turn as well a traitor too,
  Since Heaven-like pow'rs teach thee what to do?   10
  Canst not thou quite forget thy pleasures past,

Those blessèd hours, the only time of bliss,
  When we feared nothing but we time might miss,
  Long enough to enjoy what's now off cast.

---

1. iii. 427.
2. wait on] Attend on, or serve, like a lady-in-waiting at court.
3. dear sphere] The beloved, in a superior position thought of as like the
    sphere or position of a planet, above the lowly observer but inferior only to
    the Heavens above.

Leave me, vain hope, too long thou hast possessed [1]
  My mind, made subject to thy flatt'ring skill,
  While April mornings did my pleasures fill,
  But cloudy days soon changed me from that rest;

And weeping afternoons to me addressed   5
  My utter ruin, framed by Fortune's will,
  When knowledge said hope did but breed, and kill,
  Producing only shadows at the best.

Yet, hope, 'tis true thy faults did fair appear,
  And therefore loth [2] to think thou counsell'dst me,   10
  Or wilfully thy errors would not see,
  But catch at sun-motes, [3] which I held most dear,

Till now alas, with true felt loss I know
  Thy self a bubble each fair face can blow.

---

1. iii. 427–8.
2. therefore loth] Therefore I was unwilling.
3. sun-motes] Specks of dust seen floating in sunlight.

Though you forsake me, yet alas permit[1]
   I may have sorrow for my poisoned cross;
   Think not, though dead to joy, I cannot hit
Upon a torture for my soul-pierced loss,

Or if by chance I smile, I hopes engross,[2]   5
   Nor, for I die not, I do bliss admit;
   Most grief will oft give leave for show to toss
Upon the waves, where shipwrecked comfort split.

Think then your will, and, left, leave me yet more:[3]
   Vex not my loathèd life, to ruin bent,   10
   Be satisfied with glut of your bad change;

Lay me, unthought-on, in the love-killed store;[4]
   My grief's my own, or, since for you 'tis sent,
   Let me have that part from you while you range.

---

1.   iii. 428.
2.   Do not think that, if by chance I smile, that I am building up hopes ...
3.   Think whatever you wish, and, having left me, leave me even more completely.
4.   love-killed store] Among those who have died for love.

Some do, perhaps, both wrong my love, and care,[1]
   Taxing me with mistrust and jealousy,
   From both which sins in love, like freedom, free
   I live; these slanders but new raisèd are.

What though from grief, my soul I do not spare,   5
   When I perceive neglect's slight[2] face on me?
   While unto some the loving smiles I see,
   I am not jealous they so well do fare,

But doubt my self, lest I less worthy am,
   Or that it was but flashes, no true flame,   10
   Dazzled my eyes, and so my humour fed.

If this be jealousy, then do I yield,
   And do confess I thus go armed to field,
   For by such jealousy my love is led.

---

1. iii. 428.
2. slight] Disdainful.

[U44]   From a long way, and pilgrimage for love,
I[1] am returned, wearied with travel's pain,
Not finding ease, or those vexations move;
First, to my soul they are, where to remain
They vow to settle; then alas, can I   5
Think of a rest, but travel till I die.

---

1.   Sung by Pelarina, dressed as a returned pilgrim, and overheard by Perselina, daughter of the King of Macedon (iv. 449).

[U45]   Did I[1] boast of liberty?
                  'Twas an insolency vain:
             I do only look on thee,
                  And I captive am again.

---

1. Despite her cruel mistreatment, Pelarina persists in her love (iv. 453).

[U46]   Love, farewell, I[1] now discover
                Thee a tyrant o'er a lover,
                All thy promised sweets prove crosses,
                Thy rewards are only losses.

          A pretty thing I did deem thee,   5
                Innocent and mild esteem thee,
                But I find thee as curst matter
                As a swelling, high-wrought water.

          Cupid's name, a pleasant folly,
                Hath beguilèd hearts most holy,   10
                Ev'n to sacrifice in homage
                Life and soul, unto their damage.

          Mine, an off'ring once I proffered,
                Happily refused when offered,
                I'll keep now, but to revile thee,   15
                From the craft which did beguile me.

---

1. Sung by a shepherd, overheard by the reunited Pamphilia and Amphilanthus
   (iv. 482–3).

[U47]   Faithful lovers, keep from hence,[1]
                None but false ones here can enter:
                This, conclusion hath from whence
                Falsehood flows, and such may venture.[2]

---

1. A warning carved on a rock outside the Hell of Deceit, where Pamphilia can
   see Pamphilus being tortured in the flames of this hell, with his breast cut
   open to reveal her name written on his heart; her rescue attempts are beaten
   back by the flames (iv. 494–5). The episode derives partly from Spenser's
   The Faerie Queene, III. xii, where Scudamour fails to rescue Britomart,
   whose heart is cut out in the Castle of Busyrane.
2. venture] Text reads 'venter'.

[U48]   Egypt's[1] pyramids enclose their kings,
                But this far braver, nobler things:
         Virtue, Beauty, Love, Faith, all here lie
                Kept in Myra's tomb, shut from eye;[2]
         The Phoenix dies to raise another, fair,   5
                Born of her ashes, to be heir:
         So this sweet place may claim that right in woe,
                Since here she lies, Heaven willing so.

---

1. A brass plate on a pyramid in Myra, in Licia, commemorates the lady Myra,
   who died rather than give up her love for Alarinus (iv. 498).
2. Cf. Shakespeare, 'The Phoenix and the Turtle', esp. 53ff.: 'Beauty, truth, and
   rarity, / ... Here enclosed in cinders lie. / Death is now the phoenix' nest ...'.

[U49]   If a clear fountain, still keeping a sad course,[1]
            Weep out her sorrows in drops, which like tears fall,[2]
            Marvel not if I lament my misfortune,
                        brought to the same call.

        Who thought such fair eyes could shine, and dissemble?   5
            Who thought such sweet breath could poison love's shame?
            Who thought those chaste ears could so be defilèd?
                        Hers be the sole blame.

        While love deserved love, of mine still she failed not,
            Fool I, to love still where mine was neglected,   10
            Yet faith, and honour, both of me claimed it,
                        although rejected.

        Oft have I heard her vow, never sweet quiet
            Could once possess her while that I was elsewhere,
            But words were breath then, and as breath they wasted   15
                        into a lost air.

        So soon is love lost, not in heart imprinted.
            Silly I knew not the false pow'r of changing,
            Love I expected, yet (ah) was deceivèd,
                        more her fond ranging.   20

        Infant Love tied me not to mistrust change,
            Vows kept me fearless, yet all those were broken:
            Love, faith and friendship by her are dissolved,
                        suffered unspoken.

---

1. The Duke of Brunswick sings this to his lady, composed 'in manner or
    imitation of sapphics', a form of quantitative verse (iv. 512). Both Sir Philip
    Sidney and Mary Sidney had written sapphics, Philip in *Old Arcadia*, Books
    One and Three (*OA* 12 and 59), Mary in Psalm 125.
2. See Jonson's play, *Cynthia's Revels* (published 1601), I. ii. 65–9: 'Slow, slow,
    fresh fount, keep time with my salt tears; / ... Woe weeps out her division
    when she sings ...'.

[U50] That which to some their wishes' ends present,
     Is counted day, which former crosses mend,
     Yet night-like day my blessings do prevent,
     And brings that loss whereto my mischiefs tend.[1]

     By day's approach, alas, that light doth end,   5
     Which is the only light of my content,
     And more I see day strive her light to lend,
     The darker am I, by sad parting rent.

     Like one long kept in prison, brought to light,
     But, for his end, condemnèd ne'er to be   10
     Free from his dungeon till that wretched he
     Conclude his living with his latest sight.[2]

     So now with grief doth day appear to me,
     And Oh! too early, since we parting see.

---

1. The Duke of Brunswick presents this to his lady, although it was in fact
  written by his friend, the Duke of Wertenburg (iv. 514).
2. Cf. *RS* 31 ('Absence, what floods …'), 5–6: '… my life, which fettered lies, /
  And famished, dark, in prison …', and 9–10: 'For as the condemned man
  from dungeon led, / Who with first light he sees, ends his last breath …'.

[U51] Wo. Fond agèd man,[1] why do you on me gaze,
            Knowing my answer? Resolution take:[2]
            Follow not fondly in an unused maze,
            As if impossibilities to shake.
                For know I hate you still, and your poor love   5
                Can me as soon as rocks to pity move.

       Man. Alas, my dearest soul, too long I knew
            I loved in vain, your scorn I felt likewise,
            Your hate I saw; yet must I still pursue
            Your fairest sight, though you do me despise;   10
                For love is blind, and though I agèd be,
                I can nor part from it, nor it from me.

       Wo. What blame dost thou deserve, if thou wilt still
            Follow my hate, who will not breathe to change,
            And strive to gain as if from scorn or ill,   15
            Loving disdain as jewels rich and strange.
                Or canst thou vainly hope thy wailing cries
                Can move a pity? No, let this suffice.

       Man. Pity, alas, I ne'er could look to see
            So much good hap; yet, dear, be not too cruel,   20
            Though you, thus young, hate agèd love in me,
            My love hath youth, or you shall see love's fuel
                Deserving your reward; then not deny,
                Let me now see those eyes kind, or I die.

       Wo. These eyes of mine thou never shalt behold: 25
            If clouds of true disdain may dim desire,
            They shall as black be as thy faults are bold,
            Demanding what's unfit; a poor old fire
                Wasted like triumphs, sparkles only live,
                And troubled rise from embers which outlive.   30

---

1. The Dukes of Brunswick and Wertenberg overhear this dialogue, sung by an
   old man and a young woman who cannot requite his love despite his good
   qualities (iv. 515–16).
2. See *RS*'s pastoral dialogue, 'Shepherd, why dost thou so look still on me …',
   where a nymph refuses a shepherd.

Man. I do confess a boldness 'tis in me
    Ought to resist, if your sweet self command;
    Yet blind me needs you must, for if I see,
    Mine eyes must rest on you, and gazing stand:
        Heaven not forbids the basest worm her way;   35
        Hide that dear beauty, I must needs decay.

Wo. My beauty I will hide, mine eyes put out,
    Rather than be perplexèd with thy sight;
    A mischief certain, worse is than a doubt,
    Such is thy sight, thy absence my delight;   40
        Yet mine the ill, since now with thee I stay.
        Tired with all, misfortune cannot stray.

Man. Thy beauty hide? O no, still cruel live
    To me most hapless; dim not that bright light
    Which to this earth all lights and beauties give.   45
    Let me not cause for ever darkest night;
        No, no, blessèd be those eyes and fairest face,
        Lights of my soul, and guides to all true grace.

    My sweet commanderess, shall I yet obey,
        And leave you here alas unguarded? Shall   50
    I not then, for sorrow, ever stray
    From quiet peace, or hope, and with curst thrall [1]
    Sit down and end? Yet if you say I must,
    Here will I bide in banishment accurst,
        While you pass on, as cruel, happy still   55
        That none else triumph may upon mine ill.

---

1. thrall] Misery, oppression.

[U52]

1.

A shepherd[1] who no care did take
    Of aught but of his flock,
Whose thoughts no pride could higher make
    Than to maintain his stock,
Whose sheep his love was, and his care,   5
    Their good his best delight,
Their lambs his joy, their sport his fare,
    His pleasure was their sight,

2.

Till love, an envier of man's bliss,
    Did turn this merry life   10
To tears, to wishes which ne'er miss
    Incumbrances with strife.
For whereas he was best content
    With looking on his sheep,
His time in woes must now be spent,   15
    And broken is his sleep.

3.

Thus first his woeful change began:
    A lamb he chanced to miss,
Which to find out about he ran,
    Yet finds not where it is,   20
But as he passed (O fate unkind),
    His ill led him that way
Whereas, a willow tree behind,
    A fair young maiden lay.

4.

Her bed was on the humble ground,   25
    Her head upon her hand,
While sighs did show her heart was bound
    In love's untying band.
Clear tears her clearest eyes let fall
    Upon her love-born face,   30
Which heav'nly drops did sorrow call,
    Proud witness of disgrace.

---

1. Recited by the Duke of Wertenburg and composed by his lady Lycencia (iv. 520-9).

5.

The shepherd stayed, and fed his eyes,
　No farther might he pass,
But there his freedom to sight ties,　　　　　35
　His bondage, his joy was.
His lamb he deems not half so fair,
　Though it were very white,
And liberty he thinks a care,
　Nor breathes but by her sight.　　　　　　40

6.

His former life is altered quite,
　His sheep feed in her eyes,
Her face his field is of delight,
　And flocks he doth despise.
The rule of them he leaves to none,　　　　　45
　His scrip he threw away,
And many he forsakes for one,
　One he must now obey.

7.

Unhappy man, whose losing found
　What better had been lost,　　　　　　　50
Whose gain doth spring from such a ground
　Whereby he must be crossed.
The worldly care he now neglects,
　For Cupid's service ties
Care only to his fond respects,　　　　　　55
　Where wave-like treasure lies.

8.

As this lost man still gazing stood,
　Amazed at such a sight,
Imagining no heav'nly food
　To feed on but her sight,　　　　　　　60
Wishing but her beams to behold,
　Yet grieved he for her grief
When mournfully he did unfold
　Her woes without relief.

9.

His new sun rose, and rising said,   65
   'Farewell, fair willow tree,
The root of my estate decayed,
   The fruit for hapless me,
What though thy branch a sign be made
   Of labour lost in love?   70
Thy beauty doth no sooner vade
   Than those best fortunes prove.

10.

'My songs shall end with willow still,
   Thy branches I will wear:
Thou wilt accompany my ill,   75
   And with me sorrow bear,
True friend,' said she, then sighed, and turned,
   Leaving that restless place,
And shepherd who in passions burned,
   Lamenting his sad case.   80

11.

This maid now gone, alone he left,
   Still on her footsteps gazed,
And heartless grown, by love bereft
   Of mirth, in spirit raised,
To satisfy his restless thought,   85
   He after her will hie,
His ruin to be sooner brought,
   And sooner heart to try.

12.

Then thus his latest leave he took,
   'My sheep,' said he, 'farewell,   90
Let some new shepherd to you look,
   Whose care may mine excel.
I leave you to your freedom now,
   Love's laws so fast me bind
As no time I can you allow,   95
   Or go, poor flock, and find

13.

'The maid whom I so dearly love,
    Say, it was her dear sight
Which from your keep doth me remove,
    And kills my first delight.   100
Go you my dog, who careful were
    To guard my sheep from harm,
Look to them still, no care forbear,
    Though love my senses charm.

14.

'But you, my pipe, that music gave,   105
    And pleased my silent rest,
Of you I company will crave,
    Our states now suiteth best,
For if that fair no pity give,
    My dying breath shall cry   110
Through thee the pains wherein I live,
    Whereby I breathe to die.'

15.

Madly he ran from ease to pain,
    Not sick, yet far from well,
Heart-robbed by two fair eyes, his gain   115
    Must prove his worldly hell.
After his heart he fast doth hie,
    His heart to her did fly,
And for a biding place did cry,
    Within her breast to lie.   120

16.

She that refused, when he her spied,
    Her whom he held most dear,
Lie weeping by a river's side
    Beholding papers near.
Her ruling eyes must yet be dimmed   125
    While pearl-like tears she shed,
Like shadows on a picture limned;
    At last these words she read.

17.

'When I unconstant am to thee
    Or false do ever prove,   130
Let happiness be banished me,
    Nor have least taste of love.
But this, alas, too soon,' cried she,
    'Is, O, by thee forgot,
'My hopes and joys now murdered be,   135
    And falsehood is my lot.

18.

'Too late I find what 'tis to trust
    To words, or oaths, or tears,
Since they that use them prove unjust,
    And colour but our fears.   140
Poor fools ordained to be deceived,
    And trust to be betrayed,
Scorned when our hearts are us bereaved
    Sought to, a while delayed.[1]

19.

'Yet though that thou so false hast been,[2]   145
    I still will faithful be,
And though thou thinkst, to leave no sin,
    I'll make my loyalty
To shine so clear, as thy foul fault
    To all men shall be known,   150
Thy change to thy changed heart be brought,
    My faith abroad be blown.'

---

1.   Scorned when others seek to rob us of our hearts, and at other times put off.
2.   been] Pronounced (and spelt in MS) 'bin'.

20

This having said, again she rose,
  The papers putting by,
And once again a new way chose,   155
  Striving from grief to fly;
But as she going was along
  That pleasant running stream,
She saw, the sallow[1] trees among,
  The shepherd Aradeame,   160

21.

For so this woeful lad was called,
  But when she him beheld,
'What witchcraft hath thee now enthralled,
  And brought thee to this field?
What can the cause or reason be,   165
  That thou art hither come,
Where all must taste of misery,
  And mirth with grief entomb?'

22.

'If mirth must here entombèd be,
  Fair shepherdess,' said he,   170
'This place the fittest is for me
  If you use cruelty,
For know, I hither come to see
  Yourself, wherein now lies
My life, whose absence martyred me,   175
  Whose sight my power ties.

23.

'Give me but leave to live with you,
  It is the life I crave:
To you I bound am to be true,
  My life to you I gave   180
When first I did behold you lie
  In shade of willow tree:
That time my soul did to you tie,
  Those eyes did murder me.'

---

1. sallow] Willow.

24.

'Is this the reason? Ah,' cried she,   185
 'The more I wail your case,
Who thus partaker needs will be
 In grief and in disgrace;[1]
I pity you, but cannot aid
 You, nor redress your ill,   190
Since joy and pain together paid
 Scarce satisfies the will.

25.

'If I do tie you, I release
 The bond wherein you are,
Your freedom shall not find decrease, 195
 Nor you accuse my care.
The pain I have is all my own,
 None can of it bear part,
Sorrow my strength hath overthrown,
 Disdain hath killed my heart.   200

26.

'And, shepherd, if that you do love,
 This counsel take of me,
This humour fond in time remove,
 Which can but torture thee;
Take it from her who too too well   205
 Can witness it is so,
Whose hope seem'd heav'n, yet proved a hell,
 And comfort changed to woe.

27.

'For I was loved, or so I thought,
 And for it loved again,   210
But soon those thoughts my ruin brought,
 And nourished all my pain;
They gave the milk that fed belief,
 Till weaned, they provèd dry:
Their latter nourishment was grief; 215
 So famished, I must die.

---

1. Who (as true lover) will necessarily partake of grief and disgrace ...

28.

'Then see your chance, I cannot change,
    Nor my affection turn;
Disdain, which others move to range,
    Makes me more constant burn. 220
My sighs, I'm sure, cannot you please,
    My grief no music prove,
My flowing tears your passions ease,
    Nor woes delight your love.

29.

'If my sight have your freedom won, 225
    Receive it back again;
So much myself I find undone
    By gifts which prove no gain.
As I lament with them that love,
    So true in love I am, 230
And liberty wish all to prove,
    Whose hearts waste in this flame.'

30.

'Yet give me leave,' sighed he with tears,
    'To live but where you are,
My woes shall wait upon your fears, 235
    My sighs attend your care;
I'll weep whenever you shall wail,
    If you sigh, I will cry,
When you complain, I'll never fail
    To wail my misery. 240

31.

'I will you guard, and safely keep
    From danger and from fear,
Still will I watch when you do sleep,
    And for both, sorrows bear.
Make me not free, I bondage crave, 245
    Nor seek else but to serve:
This freedom will procure my grave,
    These bonds my life preserve.

32.

'For life, and joy, and ease, and all,
    Alas, lies in your hands: 250
Then do not cause my only fall,
    I tied am in such bands.
Part hence I cannot, nor love leave,
    But here must ever bide:
Then pity let my pain receive,   255
    Do not from mercy slide.'

33.

'If that,' said she, 'you constant are
    Unto your coming ill,
I'll leave this place, yet let all care
    Accompany me still: 260
And shepherd live, and happy be,
    Let judgement rule your will,
Seek one whose heart from love is free,
    And who your joy may fill.

34.

'For I love's bondslave am, and tied   265
    In fetters of disdain:
My hopes are frozen, my spring dried,
    My summer drowned with pain:
I loved, and worse, I said I loved,
    Free truth my ruin brought,   270
And so your speech the like hath moved,
    And loss for gaining bought.'

35.

With that, away she hasted fast,
    Left him his cares to hold,
Who now to sorrow makes all haste,   275
    Woes drives his hopes to fold.
Now he can see, and weeping say
    His fortune blind he finds,
A heart to harbour his decay,
    A state which mischief binds.   280

36.

This now he feels, and woefully
    His birth and life he blames,
Yet passions rule when reasons lie
    In dark, or quenchèd flames:
That place he first beheld her in,   285
    His biding he doth make,
The tree his liberty did win,
    He calls his martyr stake.

37.

And pleasingly doth take his fall,
    His grief accounts delight,   290
Freedom and joy, this bitter thrall,
    His food, her absent sight.
In contraries his pleasures be,
    While mourning gives him ease,
His tomb shall be that hapless tree   295
    Where sorrow did him seize.

38.

And thus did live, though daily died,
    The shepherd Aradeame,
Whose causeless tears which never dried
    Were turned into a stream,[1]   300
Himself the head, his eyes the spring
    Which fed that river clear,
Which to true hearts this good doth bring
    When they approach it near,

39.

And drink of it to banish quite   305
    All fickle thoughts of change,
But still in one choice to delight,
    And never think to range.
Of this sweet water I did drink,
    Which did such faith infuse   310
As since, to change I cannot think,
    Love will death sooner choose.

---

1.   An Ovidian metamorphosis; cf. that of Arethusa (*Metamorphoses* V).

[U53]   Rise, rise from sluggishness, fly fast my dear,[1]
        The early lark prevents[2] the rising lights;
        The sun is risen, and shines in the rights
        Of his bright glory, till your eyes appear.

    Arise, and make your two suns so clear show,   5
        As he for shame his beams call back again
        And drown them in the sea, for sorrow's pain,
        That you, commandress of the light, may know

    The duty sun, and all, must yield to you,
        Where richness of desert doth lie embraced,   10
        Night by your brightness wholly now defaced,
        And day alone left to you as lights due.

    Yet be as weighty still in love to me,
        Press me with love, rather than lightly fly
        My passions, like to women made to tie,   15
        Of purpose to unloose and oft be free.

    Thus may your lightness showing ruin me;
        I cannot live if your affections die,
        Or leave off living in my constancy:
        Be light and heavy too, so we agree.   20

---

1.   An aubade by the Talkative Knight, 'in commendation of his mistress's eyes'
     (iv. 538).
2.   prevents] Anticipates.

[U54]   1.

     Have I lost my liberty,
     And my self, and all, for thee
         O Love? [1]
     Yet wilt thou no favour give,
     In my loss thy blame will live;   5
         Alas, remove.

2.

     Pity claims a just reward,
     But proud thoughts are thy best guard,
         Once smile:
     Glory 'tis to save a life   10
     When deceivers are in strife
         Which to beguile.

3.

     Your gain hath my pain begot,
     But neglect doth prove my lot;
         O turn,   15
     Say it was some other harm,
     And not your still sought-for charm
         Did make me burn.

4.

     Thus may you all blame recall,
     Saving me from ruin's thrall.   20
         Then, love,
     Pity me, I'll no more say
     You to cruelty did sway,
         But loyal prove.

---

1.   Sung by Leurinius, Prince of Venice, to the shepherdess Celina, who once
     mocked love, but now suffers it (iv. 547–8).

5.

Else be sure your tricks I'll blaze,   25
And your triumph-castle raze:
    Take heed,
Conquerors cannot remain
Longer than men's hearts they gain;
    Worse will you speed.   30

6.

You a king set up by Love,
Traitors soon may you remove
    From high:
Take this counsel, serve love's will,
And seek not a heart to kill,   35
    Lest both do cry.

[U55]   Love grown proud with victory,
     Seeks by sleights to conquer me;[1]
     Painted shows he thinks can bind
     His commands in women's mind.
    Love but glories in fond loving,   5
    I most joy in not removing.

    Love a word, a look, a smile,
     In these shapes can some beguile,
     But he some new way must prove
     To make me a vassal love.   10
    Love but &

    Love must all his shadows leave,
     Or himself he will deceive,
     Who loves not the perfect sky
     More than clouds that wanton fly.   15
    Love but &

    Love, yet thus thou may'st me win,
     If thy staidness would begin,
     Then like friends we'd[2] kindly meet
     When thou prov'st as true as sweet.   20
    Love then glory in thy loving,
     And I'll joy in my removing.

---

1. Sung by a shepherdess, Lemnia, before she falls in love with Leurenius (iv. 549).
2. we'd] Text reads 'w'would'.

[U56]   This no wonder's of much weight,
          'Tis the hell of deep deceit.[1]

---

1. Amphilanthus, like Pamphilia before him (see U47), suffers enchantment in
    the Hell of Deceit; failing to rescue Pamphilia, he is expelled in a trance,
    waking to find these words written near the entrance (iv. 554).

POEMS FROM THE
NEWBERRY MANUSCRIPT
THE SECOUND PART OF
THE COUNTESSE OF
MONTGOMERY'S URANIA

Part II

[N1]   Why do you thus torment my poorest heart? [1]
Why do you clearest eyes obscure all day
From me, love's poorest vassal? Can my smart
Add triumph to your crown? Make no delay,
But quickly, O, conclude, and do not stay: 5
Rebellions must be crushed by present art.
Yet I a subject am without dismay,
For loyalty I justly claim great part,
But if those cruel eyes will not impart
A favourable censure, Oh, poor clay,   10
How can a new mould be to ease my smart?
No, a new death must all these ills repay,
Then welcome death, since by those eyes I die:
Love, look, are any clearer in your sky?

---

1.   Sung by a young prince of Corinth, in love with a vain and demanding
woman (II. i. f. 8).

Had I[1] loved but at that rate
Which hath been ordained by fate
   To all your kind,
I had full requited been
Nor your slighting me had seen,   5
   Nor once repined
   Neglect to find,

For I am so wholly thine,
As in least sort to be mine
   My heart denies.   10
I do think no thought but thee,
Nor desire more light to see
   Than what doth rise
   From thy fair eyes.

Dear, I blame not thy neglect,   15
In excess of my respect
   The fault doth rest.
Thou dost pretty love impart
As can lodge in woman's heart.
   None should be pressed   20
   Beyond their best,

But when I did give thee more
Than again thou couldst restore,
   And woman be,
I made thee against thy will   25
To remain ungrateful still,
   By binding thee
   So much to me.

---

1. Originally composed by Amphilanthus for Antissia, but intended for Pamphilia, and sung by her for the entertainment of friends (II. i. f. 10). In fact, the poem is very probably by William Herbert, Earl of Pembroke (though not included in the 1660 edition of his poems, it appears in other MSS).

[N3]   Most dear,[1] more happy sovereignsing[2] hearts,
        Free from flattering,
    Murdering pieces[3] prove your sweet eye darts
        Joys from desire scattering.

    Why, alas, were you framed, if alone to kill?   5
        You know murdering
    A crime by all condemned; is this your skill,
        Nor caused nor furthering?

    Yet you, alas, may certainly control
        Those humours flowing,   10
    But if[4] it be you love to fleet,[5] and roll[6]
        Poor slaves for honour's showing,

    Certainly you will end at last as we,
    And pity wanting, cry, alas woe's me.

---

1. Sung by a shepherdess who favours variety in lovers, but regrets the rejection of her first lover (II. i. f. 15).
2. sovereignsing] Ruling absolutely, in sovereign fashion.
3. pieces] Weapons, such as crossbows or cannon, here firing amorous looks.
4. But if] Unless.
5. fleet] Slip away or move on rapidly.
6. roll] Enrol as servants.

[N4]

Honour, now enjoy the day,
Love is fall'n into dismay,
Nay is conquered, yield all right
To the power of his might:
Honour, honour, now is all;   5
Captive Cupid sees his fall.[1]

Never let a slight love come
In honour's sight, for a doom,
Or think light affection's thrall
Dare appear, no, now 'tis gall: 10
Honour monarch is of Love,
Under him affections move.

This is Honour's purest throne,
Here he brightly shines alone,
Poor love like mean spheres appear,   15
In him's only brightness clear.[2]
Had I known him thus before,
Mine arms I had laid at his door.

Now I yield them to his worth,
This doth knowledge true bring forth: 20
Arrows, bow, darts and wings,
Which death brought to mortallings,[3]
All I offer up to you,
Dear Honour, as the monarch true.

---

1. Rodomandro, King of Tartaria (whom Pamphilia is to marry), presents a
   masque in which Honour defeats Cupid, who sings this song (II. i. f. 15).
2. Love appears like a planet or star on a lower sphere, while superior Honour
   shines brighter.
3. mortallings] Mortals.

This is Honour's holiday.[1]
Now shepherd swains, neatherds[2] play,
    Cupid wills it so.
Kings and princes, come along,
You shall safely pass from wrong,   5
    Desire was your foe.

2.

Fond desire is now laid waste,
Truth of love in his stead placed,
    Honour guides you now;
'Tis true Cupid was desire,   10
Fondly using wanton fire,
    Therefore thus doth bow.

3.

Love's not Love, that vainly flings,
Like a harmful wasp that stings;
    Therein I did miss.   15
Desire should not be styled love,
But with honour's wings to move:
    Bright love tells us this.

4.

Honour like the brightest morn
Shines, while clouded love is worn   20
    And consumed to dust,
Like fair flowers long being pulled,
Die and wither if not culled,
    Slightest like the worst.

But let hearts and voices sing,   25
Honour's Cupid's just-born king.

---

1.   The last song of the masque, when Cupid submits to Honour (II. i. f. 15).
2.   neatherds] Cattle-herders.

[N6]　　　　Come, lusty gamesters of the sea,[1]
　　　　　　Billows, waves and winds,
　　　　Like to most lovers, make your plea,
　　　　　　Say, love all combines;
　　　　Let not Dian rule your sprites,　　　　　　　5
　　　　Her pale face shuns all delights.

　　　　Venus was born of the sea foam,
　　　　　　Queen of love is she,
　　　　Like her sweet pleasant fancies roam
　　　　　　This variety.　　　　　　　　　　　10
　　　　Juno yet a firm wife is,
　　　　So may I be in my bliss;

　　　　Pallas is yet a fierce, stern lass,
　　　　　　Wisdom doth profess;
　　　　Ceres a housewife soon I pass,　　　　　　15
　　　　　　Lovers I express;
　　　　Venus, my dear sea-born Queen,
　　　　Gives me pleasures still unseen.

　　　　And you fair starry sky, behold,
　　　　　　Venus me commands　　　　　　　20
　　　　That by no means love should grow cold
　　　　　　But blow the fire brands;
　　　　Sol's best heat must fill our veins,
　　　　These are true love's highest strains.

1.　The insane Antissia, married to Dolorindus, King of Negroponte, constantly
　　composes songs and poems (II. i. f. 16).

[N7] This night the moon eclipsèd was,[1]
          Alas,
      But quickly she did brightlier shine
          Divine,
      Prognosticating by sweet rain   5
      That all things should be clear again.

      Sweet rain foretells us good to grow
          And flow,
      Cool drops sweet moisture, flowers bring
          To spring,   10
      Which fruit brings forth, and so shall we
      Live hopefully all good to see.

      But in this time the sun is lost
          And crossed,
      Though in Antipodes not quite bereft   15
          Nor left,
      But in just course shall come again,
      And with pure light both shine and reign.

---

1. Another song by Antissia (II. i. f. 16).

[N8]

Stay holy fires
Of my[1] desires,
Flame not so fast;
My love's but young,
From bud new sprung,   5
Scarce knows love's taste.

Flames should not rise
Till sacrifice
Were ready made.
A love scarce green   10
Was never seen
In with'ring shade.

Stray till 'tis blown,
If then o'erthrown
With curst denies.   15
Poor heart, swell out,
Send flames about
With murdering eyes.

Summon all men
To Court again,   20
Where Love's enthroned;
If they persist,
And smiles resist,
While chaste love is scorned,

Then spoil[2] their hearts   25
With fierce love's darts,
And with that store
Of hearts which shakes,
Make martyr stakes
Still framing more,   30

---

1. A young princess, sister of Rodomandro, sings this in a garden; Licandro,
   son of the Duke of Athens, immediately falls in love with her (II. i. f. 24).
2. spoil] Despoil, pierce.

Then with those eyes
Where all truth lies,
A blaze of fire frame,
As hecatomb
For victor's doom   35
To true love's name.[1]

So holy fires
Of my desires
May rise, and flame
Phoenix for truth   40
Consumed in youth,
Burnt to love's fame.

---

1. A sacrificial punishment in the victorious name of true love.

[N9]   Were ever eyes of such divinity
Divine?[1] No, they are of the gods.
    And so have odds[2]
Of the Gods? No, more of eternity.
They are blue, sure they are then heaven's sky: 5
    Firmly
Kings they rule and command,
Motives[3] of government do lie
    To their employ[4]
      Readily,   10
And so at mercy stand.

2.

Be they not two suns, most shiningly
Beaming? No, they are meteors rare
    Without compare.
Meteors, no? Thunderbolts killingly.   15
Were they of gods, they would deal benignly,
    Gently.
Two suns were never seen
At once: divinity
    Doth that deny   20
      Really,
But lightnings oft have been.

3.

Lightnings O no, they are enduring
And bright; are they not Cupid's eyes,
    Fallen from the skies,   25
While he is doubly blinded in alluring?
Shall I yet name them must, O then say
    You may
They are of gods, of eyes,
Of the heavens, of air most bright,   30
    Of purest light,
      Fierce sight,
Yet sweetest under skies.

---

1.   Composed by Licandro (II. i. f. 26–7).
2.   have odds] Have the advantage of, or superiority over.
3.   Motives] Directive powers.   4.   employ] Text reads 'imply'.

Fierce love, alas, yet let me rest,
Behold my boiling breast:[1]
Let me but slumber, if not sleep;
   Continually to weep
     Is too great a smart   5
      To a heart
Transformed like Niobe to wat'ry pow'rs,
       Telling hours[2]
In drops of my misfortune's art.

2.

Cruel, alas, why do those eyes,   10
Rule of the heav'nly skies,
Joy in my ruin? My poor streams'
   Flumes[3] cannot cool your beams,
     For love's sacred fire
      Must aspire   15
Transcendant to the highest pow'rs,
       Telling hours
In flames of my consuming fire.

3.

The firmament may me embrace
There wand'rers may find place   20
Transformed by love into a space,
   Borrowing of lovers' trace,
     Where continual fair
      Will tell air
We destined by force, earth, water, air, fire   25
       Bred in ire,
May yet to ev'nings fair aspire.

---

1. Sung, 'in several parts', by the waiting-women of the Queen of Argos (II. i. f. 27).
2. Telling hours] Measuring time, in water-drops.
3. Flumes] Water-streams. See the *Song of Solomon*, 8. vii: 'Many waters cannot quench love, neither can the floods drown it'.

4.

But, dull earth, I see you contend,
Not willing I ascend;
Give me then fruits of plenty here,   30
    True increase of beauty's cheer,
      Why do you create
        Such a bate[1]
To singe all hearts, by such a fire,
      And entire   35
Consuming us to our last fate?

---

1. bate] Strife, discord.

Behold, this sacred fire
In water's curstest ire
 Remains in me,[1]
Disdaining change to see,
As he makes waters touch,   5
His proud enclosing my desire,
And in his bosom keeps my fire,
While I lament too much.

2.

This lamp inflamed with love
Consumes not, yet doth move,   10
 And spends the oil,
So do I waste in toil
To climb to honours high
Which, with water and the time,
Doth the flame make higher climb,   15
And so I may rise high.

3.

But while I here admire,[2]
Water and flames conspire,
 Not yield to me,
Yet cunningly agree   20
No ease unto my burning smart,
But extinguish fiery rays,
The altar for my loving bays
To act his latest part.

4.

Time but an atom is,   25
Limited by power's bliss
 Of heav'nly might
Made by eternal right,
For heaven e'erlasting being
Makes eternity the name,   30
And me the atom of my flame,
Consumed and burnt by seeing.

---

1. Sung by Lindavera, daughter of Urania and Steriamus, when disguised as a young shepherdess (II. i. f. 36).   2. admire] Feel wonder.

[N12] Love let me live, or let me die,[1]
       Use me not worse than poorest fly
       Who finds some comfort, while alone
              I live, and waste in moan.

       I have no shrouding place from woe,   5
       The billows bear my overthrow,
       And sands they cover in disgrace
              Of my love's truest face.

       Wretch, saith the sea, here stay, and drown;
       Can you not fear her curstest frown?   10
       Alas, she chides us that you stay,
              After her just denay.[2]

       She is the goddess sole of love;
       How dare you mortal thus to move?
       Bow heart and soul to her least frown,   15
              And censured thus, lie down.

---

1. The seer Lady Mellisea appears at Queen Pamphilia's court and presents a
   masque, where a swain sings this to his beloved sea-nymph (II. i. f. 41).
2. denay] Denial.

[N13]   Love but a fancy light and vain,[1]
         Fluttering but in poorest brain,
         Birds in chimneys make a thunder,
         Putting silly souls in wonder:
         So doth this love, this all-commander,   5
         To a weak poor understander.

                          2.

         Slight him, and he'll your servant be,
         Adore him, you his slave must be,
         Scorn him, O how he will pray you,
         Please him, and he'll sure betray you.   10
         Let not his falsehood be esteemed,
         Lest yourself be disesteemed.

                          3.

         Crush not your wits to place him high,
         A thought thing, never seen by eye;
         Implore not heaven nor deities,   15
         They know too well his forgeries,
         Nor saints by imprecations move,
         'Tis but the idolatry of love.

---

1.   An old shepherd, scornful of love, sings this warning to a young sailor (II. i.
     f. 41).

[N14]   Was I[1] to blame to trust
Thy love-like tears, when 'tis most just
To judge of others by our own? While mine
From heads of love and faith did flow,
Yet fruitless ran, could I suspect that thine,   5
When in my heart each tear did write a line,
Should have no spring but outward show?

2.

My love, O, never went
In mask, which made me confident
That thine had been love too, and no disguise,   10
Not love put on, but taken in,
Nor like a scarf to be put off, which lies
At choice to wear or leave; but when thine eyes
Did weep, thy heart had bled within.

3.

But as the guileful rain,   15
The sky that weeps it doth not pain
But wears the place wherein the drops do fall,
So when thy cloudy lids impart
Those showers of subtle tears, which seem to call
Compassion when you do not grieve at all,   20
You weep them, but they fret my heart.

4.

Dear eyes, I wronged not you
To think you were as fair, so true;
Why would you then yourselves in grief attire,
With pity to enlarge my smart,   25
When beauty had enough enflamed desire
And when you were e'en cumbered with my fire?
Why would you blow the coals with art?

---

1.   Amphilanthus is grieving at losing Pamphilia (II. i. f. 50).

5.

For was less fault to leave
Than, having left, me to deceive,   30
For well you might have my unworth refused,
Nor could I have of wrong complained,
But since your scorn you with deceit confused
My undesert you have with tears excused,
And with the guilt yourself have stained.   35

Lying upon the beach,
 Below me [1] on the sands
I saw within small reach
 A lady lie in bands,
With arms across, and hands   5
 Enfolded in those twines,
Whereby a true love climbs
And for love's triumph stands.

2.

'Alas,' cried she, 'Can love
 Bequeath me no small space   10
Where I may live and love, ·
 But run in ruin's race,
Nor yet to gain death's trace?
You locks of his own hair,
Witness I still you bear   15
 In my heart's dearest place.

3.

'But O false is his heart,
 Yet faithful is his hair;
Dead is his love, a pretty art
 If we these two compare.
Hair once cut off hath share   20
With death, love's life being fled,
To shadow hair is fled,
So are my joys to care.

4.   25

'Unconstant man, yet dear,
 Behold thy hair outlive
Thy faith, thy worth, and clear
 As thine eyes, which did drive
Wrack to my heart; take back   30
These relics, lay the rack
On shrivelled hearts, and cry,
Hair outlives constancy.'

---

1. A disguised shepherd sings this to encourage Amphilanthus, still grieving
over his betrayal of Pamphilia (II. i. f. 53).

[N16]   Come dear,[1] let's walk into this spring,
        Where we may hear the sweet birds sing,
        And let us leave this darksome place
        Where Cupid never yet had grace,
           For love's bright light   5
           Must us delight,
              And Cupid's fire
              Must still respire,
        And brightest show in darkest night.

2.

        'Tis not the shades can harbour love: 10
        He lives in highest spheres above,
        And from his beams gives worlds their light,
        He reigning, crowned with sweet's delight.
           In darkness' spite
           He rules in light,   15
              For Cupid's fire
              Must still respire,
        And brightest show in dullest night.

3.

        Love doth not dwell in cold faint shade,
        Nor lurks where warm love grows to vade;   20
        He's perfect heat, and strives to move
        Where equal flames with him shows love.
           In cold's despite
           He rules in might,
              For Cupid's fire   25
              Must still aspire,
        And pow'rfull'st show in darkest night.

---

1.   Sung by Steriamus, while thinking of Urania (II. i. f. 55).

[N17]   Most happy memory, be for ever blest,
Which thus brings into my most weary mind[1]
Joys past, though others would them tortures find,
But I delighted was in them, though rest

I never felt, so was my soul distressed,   5
Yet loved the fetters did me slave-like bind.
O love, what is thy force? Some say thou'rt blind;
No, thou canst see best, and can give ease best.

Then grant my memory may with me live,
And darken not my first and dearest choice,   10
From which, though swerved, I in it still rejoice;
Nor let the fates from me those fancies drive,

For though a second love doth me enfold,
None must the former from my soul unfold.

---

1.   Steriamus, husband of Urania, is reminded of the place where he experi-
enced his first love, for Pamphilia (II. i. f. 56).

[N18]   Return, my [1] thoughts, why fly you so?
        Sorrows may my good outgo,
    Fancy's but fantastic's [2] skill,
        The soul alone hath only will.

    Heathen people had their gods,   5
        Whom they implored to have the odds
    Of mortals all, but 'twould not be,
        For love was high'st enthroned to see.

    So love of all things hath most sight,
        And nothing more than love is light;   10
    Then Cupid, take thy honour right:
        Thou'rt neither god, nor earthly sprite.

---

1.   Spoken by a young woman who had once scorned love (II.i. f. 59).
2.   fantastic's] A fantastic is one who indulges in fanciful, wild ideas.

Index of First Lines

		PAGE
Adieu sweet sun	[U4]	130
After long trouble in a tedious way	[P36]	57
All night I weep, all day I cry, ay me	[P14]	35
Am I thus conquered? Have I lost the powers	[P16]	37
And be in his brave Court a glorious light	[P80]	102
And burn, yet burning you will love the smart	[P81]	103
An end, fond jealousy: alas, I know	[P69]	91
A shepherd who no care did take	[U52]	185
As these drops fall, so hope now drops on me	[U29]	159
A surgeon I would ask, but 'tis too late	[U39]	171
Bear part with me, most straight and pleasant tree	[U5]	131
Be from the Court of Love and Reason torn	[P86]	108
Be given to him, who triumphs in his right	[P88]	110
Behold, this sacred fire	[N11]	212
Being past the pains of love	[P75]	97
Be you all pleased? Your pleasures grieve not me	[P10]	31
Blame me not, dearest, though grieved for your sake	[U25]	153
But where they may return with honour's grace	[P85]	107
Can pleasing sight misfortune ever bring	[P5]	25
Cloyed with the torments of a tedious night	[P13]	34
Come darkest night, becoming sorrow best	[P22]	43
Come dear, let's walk into this spring	[N16]	218
Come, lusty gamesters of the sea	[N6]	205
Come, merry Spring, delight us	[P93]	115
Cruel Remembrance, alas now be still	[U31]	161
Cruel suspicion, O! be now at rest	[P66]	88
Dear, cherish this, and with it my soul's will	[P30]	51
Dearest, if I, by my deserving	[P61]	83
Dear eyes farewell, my sun once, now my end	[U37]	169
Dear eyes, how well, indeed, you do adorn	[P2]	22
Dear, famish not what you yourself gave food	[P15]	36
Dear, how do thy winning eyes	[U12]	139
Dear Love, alas, how have I wrongèd thee	[U10]	137
Dear, though unconstant, these I send to you	[U35]	165
Did I boast of liberty	[U45]	177
Drown me not, you cruel tears	[U7]	133

Egypt's pyramids enclose their kings	[U48]	180
Except my heart, which you bestowed before	[P90]	112
Fairest and still truest eyes	[P62]	84
Faithful lovers, keep from hence	[U47]	179
False hope, which feeds but to destroy, and spill	[P40]	61
Fierce love, alas, yet let me rest	[N10]	210
Fie, tedious Hope, why do you still rebel	[P31]	52
Fly hence, O Joy, no longer here abide	[P33]	54
Folly would needs make me a lover be	[P72]	94
Fond agèd man, why do you on me gaze	[U51]	183
Forbear, dark night, my joys now bud again	[P4]	24
Free from all fogs, but shining fair and clear	[P89]	111
From a long way, and pilgrimage for love	[U44]	176
From victory in love I now am come	[U23]	150
Gone is my joy, while here I mourn	[U18]	145
Good now, be still, and do not me torment	[P52]	74
Grief, killing grief, have not my torments been	[P32]	53
Had I loved but at that rate	[N2]	201
Have I lost my liberty	[U54]	196
Heart-drops distilling like a new-cut vine	[U3]	129
He may our prophet and our tutor prove	[P82]	104
Here all alone in silence might I mourn	[U2]	128
He that shuns love doth love himself the less	[P84]	106
His flames are joys, his bands true lovers' might	[P79]	101
Honour, now enjoy the day	[N4]	203
How blest be they then, who his favours prove	[P83]	105
How do I find my soul's extremest anguish	[U17]	144
How fast thou fliest, O Time, on Love's swift wings	[P37]	58
How fast thou hast'st, O Spring, with sweetest speed	[P51]	73
How glow-worm-like the sun doth now appear	[P102]	125
How like a fire doth love increase in me	[P55]	77
How many eyes, poor Love, hast thou to guard	[P38]	59
How many nights have I with pain endured	[P67]	89
How well, poor heart, thou witness canst I love	[P41]	62
If a clear fountain, still keeping a sad course	[U49]	181
If ever love had force in human breast	[P48]	70
If I were giv'n to mirth, 'twould be more cross	[P45]	67
Infernal spirits listen to my moans	[U27]	155
In night yet may we see some kind of light	[P63]	85
In this strange labyrinth how shall I turn	[P77]	99
Is to leave all, and take the thread of love	[P78]	100
I, that am of all most crossed	[P59]	81
It is not love which you poor fools do deem	[P46]	68
I, who do feel the highest part of grief	[U24]	152
Juno, still jealous of her husband Jove	[P97]	120
Late in the forest I did Cupid see	[P96]	119
Leave me, vain hope, too long thou hast possessed	[U41]	173

Led by the pow'r of grief, to wailings brought | [P9] | 30
Let grief as far be from your dearest breast | [P56] | 78
Like to huge clouds of smoke which well may hide | [P99] | 122
Like to the Indians, scorchèd with the sun | [P25] | 46
Loss, my molester, at last patient be | [U33] | 163
Love, a child, is ever crying | [P74] | 96
Love among the clouds did hover | [U26] | 154
Love as well can make abiding | [P60] | 82
Love but a fancy light and vain | [N13] | 214
Love, farewell, I now discover | [U46] | 178
Love grown proud with victory | [U55] | 198
Love, leave to urge, thou know'st thou hast the hand | [P8] | 29
Love let me live, or let me die | [N12] | 213
Love like a juggler comes to play his prize | [P64] | 86
Love peruse me, seek and find | [U22] | 149
Lovers, learn to speak but truth | [P94] | 116
Love, thou hast all, for now thou hast me made | [P53] | 75
Love what art thou? A vain thought | [U13] | 140
Lying upon the beach | [N15] | 217

Most blessèd night, the happy time for love | [P65] | 87
Most dear, more happy sovereignsing hearts | [N3] | 202
Most happy memory, be for ever blest | [N17] | 219
My heart is lost, what can I now expect | [P95] | 118
My muse, now happy, lay thyself to rest | [P103] | 126
My pain, still smothered in my grievèd breast | [P68] | 90
My thoughts thou hast supported without rest | [U6] | 132

Night, welcome art thou to my mind distressed | [P43] | 65
No time, no room, no thought or writing can | [P101] | 124

O deadly rancour to a constant heart | [U38] | 170
O dearest eyes, the lights and guides of love | [P50] | 72
O memory, could I but lose thee now | [U40] | 172
O me, the time is come to part | [P57] | 79
Once did I hear an agèd father say | [P27] | 48
O pardon, Cupid, I confess my fault | [P76] | 98
O stay, mine eyes, shed not these fruitless tears | [P54] | 76
O strive not still to heap disdain on me | [P6] | 26
O that I might but now as senseless be | [U34] | 164
O! that no day would ever more appear | [P100] | 123

Poor eyes be blind, the light behold no more | [P29] | 50
Poor Love in chains and fetters, like a thief | [P70] | 92
Pray do not use these words, 'I must be gone' | [P71] | 93
Pray thee Diana, tell me, is it ill | [U15] | 142

Return, my thoughts, why fly you so | [N18] | 220
Rise, rise from sluggishness, fly fast my dear | [U53] | 195

Say Venus how long have I loved, and serve you here | [P58] | 80
Sleep, fie, possess me not, nor do not fright | [P18] | 39
Some do, perhaps, both wrong my love, and care | [U43] | 175

Sorrow, I yield, and grieve that I did miss	[P49]	71
Stay holy fires	[N8]	207
Stay mine eyes, these floods of tears	[U11]	138
Stay, my thoughts, do not aspire	[P21]	42
Sweetest love return again	[P28]	49
Sweet, let me enjoy thy sight	[P91]	113
Sweet shades, why do you seek to give delight	[P19]	40
Sweet Silvia in a shady wood	[P92]	114
Sweet solitariness, joy to those hearts	[U9]	135
Take heed mine eyes, how you your looks do cast	[P39]	60
Tears sometimes flow from mirth as well as sorrow	[U16]	143
That which to some their wishes' end present	[U50]	182
The joy you say the heavens in motion try	[U28]	156
'The spring now come at last	[P7]	27
The springtime of my first loving	[P73]	95
The sun hath no long journey now to go	[U8]	134
The sun which glads the earth at his bright sight	[P23]	44
The weary traveller who, tired, sought	[P11]	32
This is Honour's holiday	[N5]	204
This night the moon eclipsèd was	[N7]	206
This no wonder's of much weight	[U56]	199
Though you forsake me, yet alas permit	[U42]	174
Time, only cause of my unrest	[P35]	56
Truly, poor Night, thou welcome art to me	[P17]	38
Unprofitably pleasing, and unsound	[P87]	109
Unquiet grief, search further in my heart	[U32]	162
Unseen, unknown, I here alone complain	[U1]	127
Was I to blame to trust	[N14]	215
Were ever eyes of such divinity	[N9]	209
What pleasure can a banished creature have	[P44]	66
When every one to pleasing pastime hies	[P26]	47
When I beheld the image of my dear	[P98]	121
When I with trembling ask if you love still	[U19]	146
When last I saw thee, I did not thee see	[P24]	45
When night's black mantle could most darkness prove	[P1]	21
Which should I better like of, day or night	[P20]	41
Who can blame me if I love	[U14]	141
Why do you so much wish for rain, when I	[U36]	168
Why do you thus torment my poorest heart	[N1]	200
Yet is there hope. Then, Love, but play thy part	[P3]	23
You blessèd shades, which give me silent rest	[P34]	55
You blessèd stars which do Heav'ns glory show	[P47]	69
You endless torments that my rest oppress	[P12]	33
You happy blessèd eyes	[P42]	63
You pow'rs divine of love-commanding eyes	[U20]	147
You pure and holy fire	[U21]	148
You, who never ending saw	[U30]	160